SLAYING NASHVILLE

Curated by Leigh M. Clark

Aurora Corialis Publishing

Pittsburgh, PA

SLAYING NASHVILLE

Printed in the United States of America

Edited by: Renee Picard, Aurora Corialis Publishing

Cover Design: Leigh M. Clark

Paperback ISBN: 978-1-958481-36-3

Ebook ISBN: 978-1-958481-37-0

OTHER COLLECTIVES BY LEIGH M. CLARK

Slaying Southwest Florida

Slaying Tampa Bay

Slaying Atlanta

Slaying Sarasota

Slaying Chicago

The Dream is in Your Hands

The Dream is in Your Hands: She Can Do It

Living Kindly: Bold Conversations About the Power of
Kindness

Table of Contents

Introduction

The Magic of Nashville and the Women Who Slay It

Leigh M. Clark

Nashville, Tennessee, is a city that pulses with energy, creativity, and tradition. The Music City draws dreamers and doers from across the globe, with its rich history of country music, vibrant arts scene, and culinary innovation. But beyond the songs and skylines, what truly sets Nashville apart are the women who form the heartbeat of this dynamic city. These women are rising stars, entrepreneurs, and innovators who embody the spirit of Nashville—a blend of grit and grace that fuels the city's unique charm and relentless pursuit of dreams. They are the faces behind *Slaying Nashville*, the women whose stories are woven into the fabric of this remarkable city. They are women to follow, admire, and learn from, and they have authored the pages of the book you now hold in your hand.

My journey with Nashville began in 2012, while I was working for a large national deals website. We had a conference in the city, and it was an unforgettable experience. The *Footloose* reboot had just been released, and I found myself line dancing the night away at an old saloon-style dance hall, celebrating our sales successes. There was something captivating about the city, a mix of grit and glamour, much like the movie itself. My boss at the time had just been cast in a reality show called *Private Lives of Nashville Wives*, a series that aimed to compete with the popular *Real Housewives* franchise. The show focused on the lives of women in the music industry, the glamour they portrayed, and the often unseen struggles behind the sequins.

This reality show highlighted a truth I came to appreciate about Nashville: the city is a blend of tradition and innovation, where the pursuit of the American dream is very much alive, but the path to success is not always a straight line. And within this journey, the women often lead the charge, carving their own paths and setting the stage for others to follow.

The Women of Slaying Nashville: Grit, Grace, and Success

Slaying Nashville is more than just a phrase—it's a movement of women who are leaving their mark on the city and beyond. These women are entrepreneurs, creators, leaders, and rising stars, each one embodying the Nashville spirit of hard work, determination, and grace under pressure. They are the future of Nashville, and their influence extends far beyond the city limits.

Take, for example, Hannah Noel, a rising star in the Nashville music scene. As a singer-songwriter, Hannah blends traditional country roots with a modern twist, creating music that resonates with fans across genres. Her journey to success hasn't been easy—with countless nights spent performing in small venues and writing songs every chance she got—but it's this perseverance that defines the women of *Slaying Nashville*. Like many others, Hannah's story is one of resilience, of never giving up on her dreams, no matter the obstacles in her path.

Then there's Maria Brito, a woman who took hold of her life and changed her destiny. After working at an uninspiring job for more than a decade, she redesigned her entire life. She now helps women travel the world and free themselves of their own limitations. Maria stands as an example showing that with passion, creativity, and hard work, anything is possible.

These women, and so many others like them in this book, are redefining what it means to succeed in Nashville. They are the ones to follow, to admire, and to learn from. They have authored the pages of this book, sharing their stories, their struggles, and their triumphs. Their journeys are a testament to the fact that Nashville is not just a city of dreams, but a city where dreams can come true—if you're willing to put in the work.

Nashville's Growth and Demographic Shifts

Nashville's population has grown significantly over the past decade, reflecting its increasing appeal as a cultural and economic hub. In 2024, Nashville's population stands at around 687,150, with women comprising a little more than 51% of the population.[1] This demographic shift highlights the growing

---

1

https://www.census.gov/quickfacts/nashvilledavidsonmetropolitango vernmentbalancetennessee influence of women in the city, not just in music, but in business, healthcare, education, and the arts. Women like those featured in *Slaying Nashville* are at the forefront of this evolution, leading the charge in shaping Nashville's future across various industries.

The city's metropolitan area now boasts a population of over 2 million people.[2] While Nashville has long been known for its Southern hospitality and rich musical heritage, it is also becoming a diverse and cosmopolitan city. This growing diversity is contributing to the city's evolving cultural landscape, making Nashville a place where people from all backgrounds can come together to create, innovate, and celebrate.

The Spirit of Nashville: A Personal Connection

Every time I visit Nashville, I am struck by the energy and optimism that permeate the city. On a recent trip, my boyfriend and I were walking down Broadway when we encountered a woman selling newspapers to support her family of six. Despite the challenges she faced, she exuded warmth and resilience. Within minutes, we were dancing in the street with her to the sound of Freddie Jackson blaring from her iPhone. That moment captured the essence of Nashville for me—a city where music is life, where every person has a story, and where

---

[2] Executive Office of the President (July 21, 2023). "Revised Delineations of Metropolitan Statistical Areas, Micropolitan Statistical Areas, and Combined Statistical Areas, and Guidance on Uses of the Delineations of These Areas" (PDF) (Press release). Archived (PDF) from the original on July 21, 2023.

strangers can become friends over a shared love of rhythm and soul.

Nashville is a city that embraces tradition but is never afraid to innovate. It is a place where creativity thrives, where artists, entrepreneurs, and dreamers can find a supportive community that encourages them to reach for the stars. And at the heart of it all are the women of *Slaying Nashville*, who are shaping the city's future, from the musicians who fill its honkytonks with song, to the chefs who redefine its cuisine, to the business leaders who drive its economy forward.

The evolution of Nashville's industries is a testament to the city's adaptability and its ability to blend the old with the new. As Nashville continues to grow, its cultural representation is expanding, and its influence on the national stage is becoming even more pronounced. From its historical roots in country music to its current status as a hub for innovation, Nashville embodies the spirit of the American dream. And the women of *Slaying Nashville* are leading the way, ensuring that the city remains a place where dreams can come true.

The Women Who Make Nashville Shine

Nashville's history is deeply intertwined with music. Known as the Athens of the South due to its numerous educational institutions, Nashville earned its Music City nickname in the 1920s when WSM radio launched the Grand Ole Opry. The Opry remains the longest-running radio show in the United States and continues to be a cornerstone of Nashville's music scene. Over the years, Nashville has nurtured countless country music legends, from Johnny Cash to Dolly Parton, but the city's influence extends beyond country music. It has also played a significant role in the development of gospel, blues, and rock 'n' roll.

In addition to music, Nashville has become a key player in the film and television industry. The city's picturesque landscapes, vibrant neighborhoods, and historic landmarks have served as the backdrop for numerous films and TV shows, from *Walk the Line* to *Country Strong*. Nashville's thriving creative scene has attracted filmmakers and producers, drawn to the city's authenticity and the stories it has to tell. The city's investment in its creative industries is paying off, as Nashville is now seen as a viable alternative to traditional film hubs like Los Angeles and New York.

And behind many of these successes are women—women like those in *Slaying Nashville*, who are not only contributing to the city's creative industries but also leading the charge. They are the ones driving change, inspiring others, and ensuring that Nashville continues to shine as a beacon of creativity and opportunity.

A City of Dreams and the Women Who Make Them Reality

In the end, it's the people who make Nashville special. The glittery and unique individuals who bring the city to life, the women who drive its success, and the dreamers who fill its streets with hope. Each visit to Nashville reminds me of the beauty of this city, of the possibilities it holds, and of the power of music, art, and community to shape our lives in meaningful ways. And at the heart of it all are the women of *Slaying Nashville*, who are part of shaping the city's future, ensuring that Nashville remains a place where dreams can come true.

The women of *Slaying Nashville* have authored the pages of this book, sharing their stories of grit, grace, and success. They are the heartbeat of Nashville, and they are the reason this city continues to thrive. Their journeys are a testament to the fact that Nashville is not just a city of dreams, but a city where dreams can become reality.

Opening

Nicole Carver

Nicole Carver is a lifestyle manager and the CEO/founder of Carver Concierge, a boutique personal concierge and lifestyle management agency. Before starting her company in 2012, her career spanned roles as an executive-level assistant across government and corporate settings. While in those roles, she saw the desire of busy professionals to be fully present with their families and also to maintain dedication to their work. As a result, Nicole was inspired to create Carver Concierge. With teams in Tampa and Nashville, her company helps busy people focus on the things that bring them joy or make them money.

A military wife, mother of three, dog mom of two rescues, and a business owner who stays highly connected in the community, Nicole can relate to many of the challenges to maintaining life harmony that her clients face, especially those of business women.

Her company helps executives and entrepreneurs delegate their never-ending to-do lists and personal assistance tasks. Whether they're clearing the path to shatter glass ceilings in business; gaining time they haven't enjoyed in years by delegating their calendar and home management; or relaxing on luxury vacations without the stress of planning, Nicole's clients receive a discrete, caring, and high-touch concierge experience. Facebook https://www.facebook.com/CarverConcierge/ Instagram -https://www.instagram.com/carverconcierge/ LinkedIn https://www.linkedin.com/in/nicolecarver/

——

As a girl who grew up in a small, rural town in Vermont, I never in my wildest dreams imagined I'd be writing the opening for a book about women making an impact in Nashville, Tenn. I also never thought I'd become an entrepreneur, build an agency that operates in two states, or find myself featured among the amazing women of Nashville. But here I am—pinch me!

As an entrepreneur, we very seldom stop long enough to look back over our shoulder at the road that got us to where we are. We are usually so forward-thinking that the past becomes only a blur, and today is just a blip as we dash toward the future, full of ideas, inspirations, and of course, a very long to-do list. Let me share a little bit about my journey from a small town in Vermont to Nashville, and now writing this chapter.

Raised by hard-working, self-employed parents who didn't go to college, and as someone who was no more than an average student, college wasn't pushed in my direction. After high school, I landed a job as a receptionist for a Canadian hockey manufacturing company. My quick promotion to executive assistant (EA) for the VPs seemed like a success, until the day I was asked to make coffee—a task at which I spectacularly failed, was told never to do again, and soon after was let go for lacking the necessary skill sets.

Years of customer service and various levels of administrative support eventually led me back to becoming an EA again, this time for corporate and high-level state officials. This time, I was ready for the role and thrived in taking the lead, managing schedules, and finding answers to questions that stumped others. I taped a cut-out quote to my desk that said, "Do today what others won't, so tomorrow you can do what others can't." This became my mantra. I never said, "I don't know." It was always, "I'll find out and get back to you," until I became like a walking, talking Google machine filled with all the things no one knew they needed to know. This commitment to seeking answers helped me master the art of problem-solving, making me a valuable resource for the unanswerable.

Besides those tiny bumps and changes to my career path along the years, I only really saw myself working for someone else. Life was challenging enough. Widowed at 24, a single mom of two boys at 30, I was meeting the standard. Then along came this Army Special Forces officer who swept me off my feet. After a few years of dating, I quit my job and sold my house, and we packed up the kiddos and headed off to a new life in Germany. So began the adventure of a lifetime that became my 40s—marriage, living abroad, and having a baby. It was the first time that my life was not "routine," and the world seemed full of new opportunities and potential to do and be more.

Returning to the States and starting a business was the next big chapter. The path of an entrepreneur is not for the faint of heart. It can be a lonely journey of navigating the unknown, creating while trying to explain your vision, and working tirelessly while failing more than winning. However, those hard times are rewarded when you see your efforts come to fruition and know that what you provide increases the quality of life for others. In 2012, I launched Carver Concierge. Armed with a strong resolve to solve problems and a fervor for organized chaos, I devoured every bit of information that could teach me the ropes of entrepreneurship. The plan was to create a small business for personal sanity and family flexibility. I never thought it would turn into an agency spanning two states and providing services to a geographically unlimited service area.

Fast forward to 2019, and an unexpected opportunity brought me to Nashville. Although the person who invited me ended up not starting their own business, the idea of expanding Carver Concierge here felt right. Nashville was vibrant and welcoming, a place where dreams seemed just a bit more attainable. Here, I discovered a community of women leaders who not only excel in their fields but thrive by uplifting each other in every conceivable way. These remarkable women embody the essence of "all the things"—a phrase that captures their multifaceted roles as business leaders, community advocates, and dedicated friends. They don't just succeed; they excel with a spirit of abundance, leading with passion and a steadfast belief that there is always enough success to go around.

In Nashville, doors aren't just opened; they are held wide, inviting a continuous stream of new talent to step through and join in the dance of progress and mutual support. My journey to Nashville was marked by a pivotal encounter at a women's business summit, an event that changed the trajectory of my professional and personal life. Here, I connected with a network of driven, compassionate women who were not only interested in my business acumen but were equally eager to support my integration into the Nashville scene. These relationships blossomed into deep friendships and robust business partnerships, making Nashville feel more like home with each passing day.

Carver Concierge has thrived in Nashville not merely through the services we provide but through the relationships we cultivate. Each client interaction is an opportunity to extend Nashville's ethos of blending professionalism with genuine personal interest and support. Our goal has always been to not just meet expectations but to exceed them, enriching the lives of our clients by allowing them to focus on what truly matters to them.

Although I don't live full-time in Nashville, I never want to be seen as just someone who drops in to do business and dashes out. Finding ways to support and give back to the community to create friendships beyond business is important to me. I strive to be a support to others who have the entrepreneurial itch, sharing my knowledge with them in hopes of helping them fast-track the startup process and dodge a few landmines along the way to a smoother and quicker journey to profit.

Reflecting on my journey from a small Vermont town to becoming a part of Nashville's dynamic community, I am reminded of the countless ways these experiences have shaped my understanding of business and community engagement. Nashville is not just a place where dreams are pursued; it is a place where they are nurtured, supported, and realized collectively. Here, we all rise by lifting each other. Here, we all slay—not just through our achievements but in how we support each other in those achievements.

This book is more than a collection of success stories. It's a celebration of the courage and community that define Nashville's entrepreneurial spirit. As you read, I hope you find inspiration in these pages and feel encouraged to connect, dream, and perhaps start a revolution of your own.

Welcome to Nashville, where every success is celebrated as a collective triumph, and where dreams are welcomed with open arms. Here, we all rise by lifting each other. Here, we all slay— not just in what we achieve, but in how we support each other in those achievements.

Shadows to Spotlight: How My Confidence Was Unleashed

Liz Wool

Liz Wool is the founder and CEO of Public Speaking and Presentation Pros (PSP), a woman-owned business on a mission to help you speak like a pro! The firm specializes in helping entrepreneurs and women in business reach higher levels of success and visibility within their organization through effective speaking engagements and presentations. Liz is a Certified Master Trainer, Certified Instructional Designer, and Certified Training Director with three decades of experience in international corporate training and global speaking engagements. She founded PSP in 2020 and provides a speaker training curriculum charting a proven pathway to success including workshops, one-on-one coaching sessions, mentoring and support delivered live, on demand or virtual. She is an active member of the National Speaker's Association, Toastmaster's International, Association of Talent Development, and Presentation Guild and serves on the board of directors for the National Association of Women Business Owners, Nashville Chapter. Liz has earned numerous awards as a top-rated speaker on behalf of the Project Management Institute, Association of Clinical Research Professionals, Society of Quality Assurance and Johnson and Johnson Pharmaceutical Research and Development, Learning and Development. Liz earned a bachelor of science degree in nursing at the College of Notre Dame in Baltimore, Md. www.lizwool.com

―――

The businesswoman I am today, the one you'll find speaking with confidence at an immense conference or an intimate luncheon, the one who brings her joy, passion, and presence to captivate and inspire women business owners to build and grow a business and career, is unrecognizable from the person I was as a child.

As a little girl in grade school, I was petrified of speaking in front of others—let alone a group. In fact, I remember that at my parents' parties I would only talk to their friends if they asked me a question and then, respond with one word... *yes, good, you're welcome.* Just a shy child? There was so much more to this than "shyness."

I suffered from a speech impediment.

I stuttered in grade school; it was exasperating to start words and to get them out. A simple "hello" came out as, "hh-ee-ll-ooo." I was enveloped with feelings of frustration with myself, low self-worth, embarrassment, and lack of confidence. I was constantly kicking myself because as hard as I tried to say words right, I could not! Recurring thoughts of "what's wrong with me?" resided in my soul and spirit daily. On top of that, I was laughed at by a few schoolmates, which pulled me inward, into my shell. These experiences left me feeling insecure and sad. Sometimes I cried because I could not talk "right."

The bright light came when I changed schools in second grade, with the blessing of a talented, kind, and patient speech therapist who worked with me once a week throughout grade school; the aim was to graduate from speech therapy before I entered middle school. I overcame my stuttering and gained superb insights as to why and when I would stutter. I was also provided with the mental, emotional, and speaking tools, but I remained shy and fearful of speaking in front of a room full of people—even as I grew into an adult.

During my medical research career, I was caught off-guard when asked to give a presentation for work in a hotel ballroom, in front of 400 people. I was feeling very nervous and anxious, and the fight-or-flight feeling came over me. I tried to fight it... *HECK NO! NO! NO! NO!* After taking a few deep breaths and talking to myself, saying, "breathe, it is okay, it is only 10 to 15 minutes, how hard can it be?" I was determined that I was not going to mess up this chance to be seen and recognized in my job and by management, and I accepted that I had to give the presentation. I realized that I needed to deliver this presentation for ME—not only was it expected for my job, it provided me the visibility to move up in my career. It also brought me out the shadows of fear and shyness and into the spotlight.

Going into this presentation, I practiced 100 times; in the shower, while walking, while driving, in my office. I did a practice run with fantastic managers who supported me. I focused on the techniques I learned in grade school to overcome my stuttering, which was the REASON FOR MY FEAR of public speaking. I said the words correctly, recited the content accurately, and sounding correct, I knew my talk from beginning to end! I was confident! I knew that I could give this talk. I was a bit nervous, but not crazy nervous!

The room for my presentation was MASSIVE! I had never seen a room this BIG. Four ballrooms wide. A twisted feeling in my stomach along with nausea and pervasive anxiety washed over me. When my name was called to present, I reminded myself that I was the expert who is presenting vital information to help them. *I can do this*, I thought, *I can walk into and through my fear for the audience and for ME*, to serve us both. I was motivating myself to come out of my shadows to shine!

I walked up focusing on feeling and looking confident. However, inside I felt a big knot in my stomach, I felt so anxious that my stomach was upset, but, not quite to the point of nausea! I was ready with my slide handouts, a pad of paper, pen, and a *paperclip*. I took the pen and the paperclip with me because I knew my anxiety could be alleviated by rubbing them fervently while presenting. This turned out to be a great idea because I presented behind a TALL podium (the top came up to my chest level). Because I could rub my fingers on that pen or paperclip, I was able to stay poised at the microphone. I began my talk with an off-the-charts level of fear, which dissipated in about five minutes, but the nervousness never went away. Weirdly, my right thigh shook uncontrollably until the end of my talk. I was sure that everyone could see my shaking leg! I slapped my right leg discreetly a few times so the audience would not see me!

After the talk, I realized that I hadn't stuttered! My reason for not wanting to be in the SPOTLIGHT had been eradicated. My confidence exploded! I realized I could *do this*! I faced my nerves and fear, walked into it, through it, endured it, and finished strong!

I learned that building my confidence took time, focus, commitment, and being comfortable with the uncomfortable in public speaking. And, knowing the reason for my fear and using the techniques that worked for me. I realized that nervousness is personal, and each person needs their own plan to overcome their fear and anxiety. This was the critical first step in having faith and KNOWING that I could do things that are hard!

I discovered that I am resilient! I can make an impact and difference in the midst of my fears, and grow confidence at the same time.

Harnessing my newfound confidence and success, I transitioned into corporate training roles and nervously submitted applications to speak at medical conferences... I was accepted! These conferences have taken me around the globe, across the United States and into Canada, Europe, Japan, and India. Some rooms had 800 people in attendance. Speaking at these conferences helped me discover a key principle to improving presentation skills: Listening to great public speakers at conferences!

I intently observed these speakers and became a student of their captivating techniques and styles. Hooked, I joined speaker associations to learn the art and craft of developing and delivering compelling, captivating presentations. What emerged from years of refining and improving my public speaking craft and skills was my "inner thespian." This is in all of us, waiting for the right guidance and support to unleash it. I found that when speakers utilized intentional vocal variety, body language, facial expressions, and intentional stage placement of their bodies, they connected with their audience and made a bigger impact.

I also discovered that walking the stage was a natural way to relieve stress and channel my nervousness into energy that draws audiences into the talk. No more fidgeting with pens and paperclips! Intentionally walking the stage became my "signature" technique, while other speakers stood behind a podium!

As my confidence and skills grew, I was able to focus on crafting presentations customized to audiences—the reason every speaker is <u>invited</u> to speak.

Speaking at international conferences empowered me to launch two successful medical research consulting and training companies. I knew that to build my brand, create name recognition, and grow my visibility, *I chose not to be the best-kept secret!* I had to be on stage to showcase my expertise, give a compelling presentation and delivery style that connected with people and inspired them to implement recommendations that I gave in my talk. The most rewarding feedback I received was from an audience member who came up to me a few years after she attended a talk of mine at a conference. She shared that it was a great talk and that my stories were fabulous because one of those stories happened at her company. She knew exactly what to do to address the situation. This is the joy in why I love to help people through public speaking.

I was able to launch and grow two businesses based on effective, compelling public speaking engagements, and I now help women in business understand their nervousness. I zero in on solutions for them (like I did for my stuttering), share their greatness, and increase their visibility, which then helps them build their careers and/or business. I guide women in business to come out of their shadows and into the SPOTLIGHT to harness their confidence, achieve their dreams, visions, and goals for next-level impact and success. I help them create successful mentoring and coaching programs, as well as workshops, by bringing their talents and uniqueness to their audiences. I help them connect with audiences and reach next-level success, just like I have!

Recently I supported two women in Nashville with their presentations. One was a university student who refined her pitch talk for an entrepreneurial grant. Her presentation was to judges from the local business community. When I spoke to her afterward, she said my feedback was critically helpful, giving her the courage to share her personal story for the first time and nuances in her message. I helped her find her voice and increase her visibility to achieve HER goal of winning first place for the grant; when I found out she won it, I jumped for joy! We are still in contact today. She is on the path to incredible achievements, and I am proud to have played a small part in her journey!

The other woman has a professional services business. She shared that she's presented her talk many times, however she wanted people to move from asking her questions to booking calls with her for business growth. She shared with me that my insights, targeted areas to enhance messaging, slide visuals, and focus on what the audience want help with, supported her in achieving the goal. After I helped her, she started booking calls!

For women in business, finding our voice, elevating our visibility to build our careers and business to reach our dreams and goals and creating a legacy, begins with harnessing your passion to make an impact; the world needs your voice and talents!

Quoting Gaye Hendricks' book the *Big Leap*, you are able to embrace your Zone of Genius attributes and qualities to inspire the vision, plan, and legacy of your business. Women are smart, creative, and innovative and have unique solutions for our clients, customers and organizations!

Shifting from the shadows to the spotlight with public speaking provides IMMEDIATE access to your future. It allows the audience to authentically connect with you one-on-one. They get to know you, who you are, your Zone Of Genius, your likability and credibility as the person who can help them.

Becoming comfortable and confident and sharing your Zone Of Genius with an audience can be learned, as I have shared with you in this chapter.

I want to INSPIRE you so YOU can learn to attain confidence in public speaking and craft and deliver a winning talk or presentation that allows your audience to connect with you, catapulting your business growth and your career opportunities.

And remember, YOU are YOUR brand, and people work with people they know, like, and believe are credible!

This is YOU!

I am inspired by Jim Rohn's quote: "Give whatever you are doing and whoever you are with the gift of your attention."

When you are 100% present for your talk or presentation, YOU lead people to connect with and experience you, and they will want to work with you.

They see the AMAZING YOU!

Cancel me, baby.

Taylor Ferber

"Don't tell me what I can and can't say." Veteran entertainment journalist Taylor Ferber wrote this in her unprecedented *Playboy* feature she spearheaded, challenging the notion that brains and beauty are mutually exclusive. She's the only woman who both posed and was a featured writer in the same issue of the iconic publication.

Taylor reinvented red carpet reporting for years as Hollywood's "Celebrity Whisperer." She interviewed and humanized the biggest A-listers like Oprah, Chris Pratt, Kim Kardashian, Lady Gaga, Mark Wahlberg, and Scarlett Johansson, at every major event from the Oscars to the Grammys and MTV Awards. Using a selfie stick, Taylor went beyond the tired "Who are you wearing?" questions for real interactions with the stars like we'd never seen them.

Her cutting edge show, "Talk To Me Taylor" (formerly "Cancel Me, Baby!"), gives an irreverent view that empowers audiences to think freely outside rules around culture, media, politics, and their daily lives. Taylor's unique style showcases our culture's most influential entertainers and thought leaders (like Josh Duhamel, Dave Portnoy, Tucker Carlson, and DeuxMoi) to be who they are and say what they really think.

Taylor's work has been published in outlets like *USA Today*, *NY Magazine*, *HuffPost*, *Us Weekly*, Fandango, and Bustle, and she's been featured on NPR, Fox News, and Barstool, for her pull-no-punches take on timely and controversial topics. Her show name may have recently changed, but her mantra remains the same: Cancel me, baby.

https://www.instagram.com/talktometaylor/
https://www.youtube.com/@TalkToMeTaylor

———

Have you ever gotten in trouble with an A-lister like Blake Shelton, a TV network, and an entire PR company simultaneously? No?

Well don't worry, I got you covered.

I didn't mean to. And I didn't expect this just a few short months after being fresh on the scene for a new start in Nashville. I mean, it's not like I was a rookie. By then I'd already been doing red carpet reporting *my* way for eight years, had a bout when a very famous A-lister tried to very publicly get me canceled, had editors try to manipulate my point of view (or flat-out reject my work), and experienced all the slap-on-the-wrist time outs and questioning-life-purpose existential crises in between.

I don't follow the rules set out for me... so sue me. After all, this is Nashville, the mystical land of trucks and whiskey and boot-scootin' fun!

Or so I thought.

Here I was, backstage at Blake's establishment Ol' Red, smack dab on Broadway, taking the gold in the Awkward Olympics. You see, Blake was at his famous Nashville bar promoting his new slapstick game show, surrounded by fellow celebs and reporters with fancy, shiny camera crews. All par for the course. I, on the other hand, was armed with nothing but a selfie stick as per the unorthodox interview style I'd invented on the Hollywood red carpet and used for years to disarm and humanize countless A-listers for interactions that were real and more interesting.

Well, USA Network had other plans.

The selfie stick was a hit. Blake and I had a totally engaging interaction about our divisive culture, and he had a genuinely thoughtful yet diplomatic response. No one cares about who can toss a horseshoe the best anyway (which I later told the publicity pack, in my defense). Give the people what they want. That's my motto.

We said warm goodbyes, I played a ring toss with Carson Daly while an amused Blake spectated, and went on my way.

Shortly thereafter, my whiskey neat and I were ambushed by the powers that be for going rogue, as they insisted I publish *none* of the footage. Why? Because he referenced politics. GASP. Thus, I'm DOA. Both intimidated and annoyed by the nonsense, I made a deal that we'd decide together what would run, which ultimately led to the backstage prosecution that could give *Depp v. Rose* a run for its money. His personal representative and aforementioned suits had me watch through the interview I'd just done with him frame by frame—the whole entourage of police hovering over me like the IRS come tax season.

For what it's worth, they were all cracking up at the footage until they realized they were there to punish me and instantly went Miss Trunchbull on my ass. Give the people what they want worked, if you ask me.

I didn't choose the "cancel culture" life—it chose me.

Don't get me wrong. It's not like I sought out a career in entertainment just to be a ballbuster. Since I was a kid, I had a deep fascination with human psychology and dialogue, namely getting into the minds of those with great influence and power. I can say that I've accomplished that in ways beyond my wildest dreams. I've been published in countless mainstream outlets, interviewed almost every A-lister, been flown around the world to report from blockbuster movie sets, and now do a popular podcast.

I learned early on that stepping out of line wasn't for the faint of heart. The "man" and powerful establishments don't like what they can't control... which is all the more reason to push up against them.

A defining moment in my career came out of nowhere like the overnight fame of the Hawk Tua girl. I called Chrissy Teigen out in a piece for being a hypocritical cyberbully. She didn't like it. She came after me on Twitter, which led to VH1 taking down the piece and suspending me. I was 25 and thought my career was over. I was convinced Chrissy Teigen would literally sue me for the whopping $2,000 I had in a bank account.

I was at a fork in the road. Either I keep my head down and appease Chrissy and VH1—or I stand by my words, which I fiercely believed in. With barely any money, no job prospects, and two friends in my new city of LA, I walked away.

Maybe it was divine intervention from the spirit of Joan Rivers, but because I quit VH1, I got my first red carpet reporting gig. So I took another risk. The "right" way to do red carpets was: look squeaky clean, be boring, and ask about their clothes. I went another way—and that's when my platform Talk

To Me Taylor (https://www.youtube.com/@TalkToMeTaylor) and the selfie stick interview was born.

Despite all the great selfie stick moments like Michael Douglas grabbing my nose, or Danny DeVito joking about how his head was at my boob level, I constantly came up against powerful entourages, studios, and execs who were threatened and alarmed by their unfamiliarity in what I was doing.

Nevertheless, I kept going. And took another chance.

Ever since high school, I wanted to pose in *Playboy*—but also be among the great writers whose work was published in the magazine. I was fascinated by how revolutionary and fearless the publication was and by the sheer power of the women on display in their ultimate feminine beauty and untouchable magnetism.

So in 2018, I did both. I spearheaded a *Playboy* pictorial featuring me and other female journalists, and I wrote an essay on free speech, detailing my journey as a reporter and fight against censorship. It wound up being a six-page spread in *Playboy*'s 65th Anniversary Issue dedicated to freedom of expression, and I was featured in the front Playbill as a contributing writer.

The real reason I did it was to prove that professional women can and should live freely in both their intelligence and sexuality, and despite deep societal beliefs, the two aren't mutually exclusive.

To this day, I'm the only woman who both posed and was a featured contributor in the same issue.

When the pandemic took out Hollywood, that's when I decided to move to Nashville. And that's when I embarked on the mission to sculpt and carve the body of my dreams. It changed everything. With true discipline and focus, I learned from experts, was in the gym two hours a day, and completely changed my diet. Just call me a Patrick Mahomes protégé.

I had an energy, confidence, buzz, lust, vitality, and power I'd never experienced before. I also started dressing like a real-life Barbie (loving every minute of it) and even started ditching bras. In Pam Anderson we trust.

What I soon discovered was that it was about so much more than what I looked like or my body. It was about my true potential and power—the power of refusing, truly refusing, to be put in a box.

Our politically correct society prides itself on breaking people out of said boxes. I believe people—on both sides—truly haven't gotten around to this one yet when it comes to successful women. To hell with 'em.

Boobs out, brain out. That's my latest motto.

This is risky. I risk how it'll be received by professionals and even family. I risk not being taken seriously in business, political conversation, culture, or media. I risk being torn down, even by fellow women.

But I'll tell you this. I've since had conversations on my platform with some of our culture's most prominent and influential leaders—from science to politics, tech to pop culture, art to business. I've talked to Dave Portnoy, NatGeo reporter

Mariana van Zeller, Tucker Carlson, TV star and activist Dr. Sheila Nazarian, and the massive podcaster DeuxMoi. I've talked to the legendary journalist Matt Taibbi about exposing the "Twitter Files" alongside Elon Musk. I've talked to world-renowned scientist Dr. Robert Malone (who went viral on Joe Rogan) about being censored on a massive scale. I talked to Josh Duhamel about releasing his latest politically incorrect movie in an over-sensitive culture that he said needs to "lighten up."

Did I mention I did all of this as braless Barbie?

They tell you to go one way. Do yourself a favor and go the other.

By the way, the Blake Shelton situation worked out just fine. His publicist, in fact, opened the door for a more appropriate place and time for an in-depth sit-down interview with Blake, Bill Maher style, if that's what I wanted.

Look out, Bill.

The Method of *Real* Healing

Vanessa Bentley

Vanessa is a licensed professional counselor (LPC) serving the Nashville and broader Middle Tennessee communities. Before becoming a psychotherapist, she earned a B.F.A in Musical Theater from the Tisch School of the Arts at New York University and worked in theater, film, television, and print modeling for ten years. From the professional stages of Manhattan to the historical stages of Europe, including a European tour of *West Side Story* in the role of "Maria," her work as an actress brought her to both coasts of America and across oceans. After ten years, she transitioned careers, earning an M.A. in Counseling from Trevecca Nazarene University in Nashville, Tenn. She cut her teeth in the field in a community nonprofit, servicing underprivileged clients throughout Middle Tennessee. Vanessa's career expanded as she began to lecture and teach counseling students, divinity students, and clergy on the intersection of psychology and theology. Vanessa has lectured at Vanderbilt University, Lipscomb University, Nashota House Seminary, Sewanee: the University of the South, Cumberland Heights addiction treatment center, and more. In 2021, she expanded her reach by publishing her first book, *The Toolbox: The Tools We Need to Build Relationships and Repair Them When They Break* and launching her podcast, *Substance, Not Psychobabble*. Vanessa's voice is currently heard in 78 nations around the world, and her message is simple: "Your soul work is to discover who you *truly* are and learn how to love that human being."

Instagram: @vanessathetherapist

X: @vthetherapist

LinkedIn: Vanessa Bentley, LPC

———

I was raised to be a liar.

Don't get me wrong... I wasn't rewarded for outright lying. Not directly anyway. But I *was* raised to pursue high standards, impossibly high at times, and when I couldn't meet them, I wasn't exactly punished for faking it, exaggerating my achievements, or presenting myself as further along the road than I actually was. As long as the deception aligned with my parents' vision for me, I was rewarded with approval and praise.

Appearance mattered more than authenticity.

So, I lied. About nearly everything.

I took piano lessons for many years but didn't practice, so I wasn't very good, but when my parents talked about my piano playing, they said I could play Beethoven and Mozart. I didn't correct them; I was a child. When I claimed the same thing, they didn't correct me either.

When I was cast as a featured extra in *The Stepford Wives* (Paramount Pictures, 2004), the family narrative was that I was now on the Hollywood A-list.

When I landed my first professional theater gig, the lead role, in an off-off-Broadway theater, the family narrative was that I had (almost) made it to Broadway!

For us, the truth was malleable as long as the embellishments fit the family narrative. We fibbed, exaggerated, and "amplified" reality to paint a picture that we were *extraordinary*. Being ordinary wasn't an option in my home; you had to be *extraordinary*. *Extraordinarily* smart, *extraordinarily* successful, *extraordinarily* impressive.

I tried hard. And when real life didn't quite match the dream, I fibbed it up to par.

I lived in a constant tension that was normal to me. I craved acceptance but lived in shame. I craved safety but lived in fear. Every day, I was afraid that my lies would be discovered—they were, so I concocted more lies to cover the lies I'd already told. I was always negotiating the distance between what I was *supposed* to be and what I *actually* was, with shame and fear filling the gap. By the time I was a teenager, I had a dual personality: the good church girl and the secret rebel, the good student and the cunning cheater. I had a charming, beloved persona I showed my parents and other adults, and a ruthless, calloused side that only came out when I thought no one was watching.

I moved to Manhattan to attend the Tisch School of the Arts at New York University when I was 17 years old. Going from a mid-sized town in New Jersey to the Big Apple was a humbling experience. I went from being the "big fish in a small pond" to a virtual nobody overnight. Some of my classmates were already on Broadway. Some had been childhood television and film stars. Their recognizable faces and triple-threat talents were... *extraordinary*. All of a sudden, the standing ovations I'd graciously accepted at the end of sold out high school performances seemed laughable.

This pattern of minimizing myself in comparison to others was an essential part of my internal motivation: I used shame as a whip on my back. When I felt small, I only worked harder. When I did succeed, and ironically I did often, I couldn't enjoy it. The carrot stick dangling in front of me was perfection, not success. Little wins were torture; they only reminded me that I wasn't "there" yet. I wasn't at the top of my game, on the top of the world. Small successes, instead of being seen as stepping stones and important lessons, were reminders that I was still a failure.

I booked my first commercial audition and more after that.

I booked my first feature film audition and more after that.

I joined the Screen Actors Guild as a junior in college.

I started working professionally in the lead role of a new musical as a senior in college.

I booked the lead role in a European tour right after graduation.

I won awards.

None of it was enough. I kept the carrot stick way out in front of my nose. While my professional accomplishments mounted, my mental health deteriorated. Outwardly, I was climbing the ladder of the theater world; inwardly I was collapsing under the pressure I put on myself. At 23, when the lies, shame, and fear came to an excruciating head, I made a phone call to a therapist that changed the course of my life.

"Hello, my name is Vanessa," my voice trembled on a stranger's answering machine, "I need someone to call me back as soon as possible."

Mary called me back that day, and I went to see her the next. As soon as the door closed behind me and I sunk down into that soft, worn-out chair, I broke down crying; I didn't stop for six months. The dam had broken, and *years* of shame, fear, and alienation poured out of me in a river of tears. For the first time in my life, I received empathy and compassion.

Therapy is a million moments, most of them unmemorable, but breakthroughs are why people go, and when we are painfully honest in therapy, those come rather regularly. One session was particularly poignant. I dropped into my chair, gazed at the Empire State Building outside the window of her office, drew in a deep breath, and declared,

"I know why I act."

"Why, Vanessa?"

I turned to face her.

"Because when I'm up there, people listen to me. They have to. They *paid* to. It's the only place in my life where I actually feel heard."

And as I processed my motivation for acting—ego, not art—I knew my acting career was over. Ego wasn't enough; I wanted something real. I was starting to tell the truth for the first time in my life, and as I did, my path was beginning to take shape. I didn't realize it at the time, but in Mary's office, my quest for success at any cost transformed into a pursuit for authenticity.

When I asked her one day, "Mary, do you think I could do what you do?"

She looked at me and smiled, "Vanessa, I think you'd be a *marvelous* therapist."

I moved to Nashville in March of 2009, still clinging to the dream I was supposed to have: being a star, this time as a singer-songwriter. Within a few short months, I had a manager, meetings at the top labels in town, and some key players were starting to make plans for me. I sat in the office of the head of A&R at one of the most famous record labels in the world, dressed to look the part, saying all the right things, with a sinking realization growing inside me: *I don't want to do this anymore.* I graciously thanked everyone for their time, walked outside into the late spring sunshine on Music Row, and quit.

I quit the facade of the person I was supposed to be.

I quit the pursuit of a talent that wasn't my passion.

I quit the path that had been set in motion by my ego and the fear of being ordinary.

I quit *lying*.

I found a new therapist in Nashville, and in my first session—by this time in graduate school for counseling and fancying myself an old pro at this—I threw out a challenge,

"I'm going to give you my life story in ten minutes."

"Go!" he said.

The minutes flew by as I covered 30-something years of history, summarizing the major themes and important memories, and at the point in my story when the lies caught up with me I described it this way,

"Everything I thought I was shattered."

He interrupted me with seven potent words: "*Best* thing that ever happened to you."

What? I thought. *Being shattered was the "best thing" that ever happened to me?*

I'd come to appreciate the power of truth, but from that moment on, I began to understand the purpose of pain. Two life lessons became personal values that have become professional hallmarks:

1. Tell the truth and face it.
2. Let your pain transform you.

Therapy is useless if it does not accomplish these two objectives, and yet, so many pursue therapy to hear what they want to hear so they can feel less pain. Likewise, many therapists talk people out of their pain by colluding with the lies they tell themselves.

The reduction of pain is an outcome of therapy, not the goal. The goals of therapy are (1) making a commitment to the truth at all costs and (2) facing the fear of ourselves, the light *and* the darkness. We don't become mentally healthy with a diagnosis, venting sessions, and a pill. Mental health is simply making a commitment to tell the truth and thus live in reality, *as it is*. It's learning to prioritize authenticity over appearance. It's accepting that we are indeed ordinary *and* extraordinary. And it's learning, slowly, how to love ourselves unconditionally.

My Great Escape

Maria Brito

Known as the Retreat Creatress, Maria's healing journey started in 2000, and as she started feeling the transformative power yoga had in her life, she felt inspired to share it with others. In 2012, she completed a 200-hour yoga teacher training in New Mexico. In 2013 she completed her life-coaching certification and started to blend different modalities as she worked with women. Her husband's military career led them to live in various places in the Middle East and Europe, which expanded the levels of training she could access, inspiring her to create workshops and programs for women only.

In 2018, she started her 500-hour yoga certification training and in 2020 completed her Tantra & Kundalini yoga certification. She continued to explore more healing modalities and added breathwork and somatic work to her perfectly curated four- to five-day escape retreats. These retreat experiences transport women to fabulous and exotic places throughout the world for them to disconnect from the world so they can connect with themselves.

Maria has a gift for creating experiences where she coaches and teaches women much-needed tools for healing; in this, she creates a safe space for women to explore the deep meaning of all their experiences. Each workshop is crafted in as a way to trigger important questions within the self, as well as inspire them to create and manifest.

So many lives have been transformed with the tools that Maria teaches. Her mission is for all women to understand their self-worth, connect to the divine power that lies within, and become the Creatress of the magnificent life they desire.

Head over to her Instagram (@awakenwithmariabrito) or Facebook (Awaken with Maria Brito) to find testimonials from women around the world and read how Maria's coaching has helped them transform and awaken their divine power.

Website: www.AwakenWithMaria.com/WellnessRetreats

––––

I get asked all the time, "Maria, what led you to this work?" My answer is simple:

I was fed up.

Simple...yet not so simple!

Beneath those four words, there are many layers of complicated issues that took me years to unravel.

You see, I said *enough is enough* after realizing that I had been living my life asleep, and I was tired of the escapism game I kept playing; in trying to escape my own life, I kept numbing myself so I would not feel what was really going on in my mind, my heart, or my crippled soul. I could eat the pain away, drink the pain away, smoke it away, and "busy" it away so I had no time...which meant giving myself full permission to ignore it away too. I was slowly losing myself until that blessed day when I looked at myself in the mirror and realized I didn't know who was staring back at me.

That was the day that kicked off my radical personal development journey.

I think back on that day and I smile now, because I know it was the day of my awakening, the day I woke up from self-loathing.

I am who I am today because of the choice I made that day.

The more I share this work with the world, I see how many women are trying to survive instead of feeling like they are thriving. I like to remind women that they can have the most amazing life and that they have the power to thrive day in and day out. But this requires work and one simple choice: You must choose yourself and put yourself first!

And the answer that I get back time and time again is: *But how?*

I know this is probably one of the hardest things to ask any woman who has children or is in a relationship with a partner, because we have been programmed to be selfless. It has been preached left and right that if a woman puts herself first, she's being selfish. And yet there is that famous saying, "If mama ain't happy, no one's happy," right? Well, it's true, and I'm here to normalize this radical way of thinking. I'm here to remind women of their worth, and this is why I decided to create the most magical experiences so that women could escape to find themselves. I now like to say that I am my best, the highest version of myself when I'm escaping!

My retreats are meant to help women escape their "normal" and bring them to a place of total self-awareness. I create and lead them because in my own life, that's what it took for me to realize that I was living life for others and not for myself, and that finally something needed to change.

It was during a women's retreat that I experienced many breakthroughs after many breakdowns, and I left with a brand new perspective on how I needed to live my life. After that retreat, I realized that I needed to make some changes. And after some deep experiences and self-revelations, I finally realized that I was simply scared of facing my greatness, and that fear is what kept me small and not playing in life fully. After that retreat, I made a promise to myself that I would create a new normal and that I would face my fears, witness them, and hold myself through it all. And I did! Shortly after that, I hired a life coach and began my journey in creating my life by design—the life I always wanted and was too scared to claim.

I wanted a life full of ease and excitement, so I created a list of all the things I wanted to experience. One by one, I wrote out my fears about these manifestations. What could possibly happen once I reached a goal? What would it require from me, and how would it be perceived by others?

I quickly noticed that I had not allowed myself to reach any of those goals because I still believed an old story that was playing in my head. And so, I had to also get clear on how each of those stories would emerge... were my fears based on my own beliefs, or someone else's?

You know what I realized? All those limiting beliefs were not really mine! I had taken them on as my own and it was time to let them go.

We must believe in our greatness, and that the world needs what we have to offer. We have each been given a divine gift to share with the world, and it is up to us to be brave enough to step into the light and shine. No more hiding! And this is what happens at my retreats, women shed layers upon layers of programming. They start to take radical responsibility to be in the right relationship with the women they desire to be...and whoa, that desire, that determined spirit is the energy that starts shifting things for the better.

Imagine 20 women with this same desire and determination in one amazing space! That is what the retreat brings, and this is why it works so effectively. It is hard to find spaces that hold this kind of magic in the outside world.

I was asked once in a training to write my own obituary explaining the kind of legacy that I wanted to leave behind. As I wrote it out, I realized what a big responsibility we all have. We must build the courage to leave our mark by being unapologetic about showing the world who we are and what we bring. And it also made me so sad to realize how so many are too afraid to leave their imprint in this world.

A couple of nights after I finished my assignment, I had a dream that I attended my own funeral, and one by one, all the women that I had helped so far stepped forward. It was a celebration, and it felt like a retreat. All the women were wearing white, all were radiant, and each shared how, because of me and my example, they were able to claim their power and live the life they always wanted. In awe of my own dream, I witnessed them all like a proud mama, and danced around them, my heart filled with immense joy.

And that, my friend, is what I want for you too! I want you to look back at your life and say, "I did that!"

Today, I can proudly say that I have witnessed many women finally busting through fear and doing the thing that at one moment in their lives kept them crippled in fear. I'm sure you know someone who is not living out their fullest potential—and maybe that someone is you. I'm here to remind you that we need you to step up and show us what you've got! I'm also here to tell you that you may need to escape to find the courage to show up.

Take the leap of faith. If you mess up a bit along the way, know that this too will build character.

I will leave you with these little nuggets that I hope you never forget:

1. Don't let failure stop you. The fact that you fail means you get to try again, and this time, you'll show them that you can come back stronger, wiser, and more determined than ever.

2. You are not for everybody, so don't try to please everyone. Be your most authentic self, and those who are not meant for you will fall away. This makes space for those who you are meant to meet.

3. Vulnerability connects us. Be brave enough to show the world you are human, and know that it is okay to show emotions. Don't apologize for tears, and remember that when you are vulnerable, you are giving others permission to feel it all.

4. Celebrate yourself. In all your wins, you are acknowledging all the past versions of you that stumbled and wanted to quit but didn't. By celebrating yourself, you are celebrating your five-year-old self, your teenage self that struggled to be loved, and the 21-year-old you that felt so lost. Your life is a celebration!

I can admit that as I've gotten older, I have realized many things about myself. Age does aid in gifting you immense awareness, but having the courage to bring things to the light and talk about them honestly changed everything for me. As I stopped the wrong kind of escaping even in the smallest things, I started to pay attention to what I kept avoiding and asked myself why.

If you are still reading, then I must have said something that tugged at you and kept you wanting more. Don't forget that there is greatness on the other side of the threshold, and that you might possibly look back and wish you had taken the brave step sooner. Most times, what lies on the other side is really not as hard as we made it out to be.

May these words create a powerful shift for you!

With fierce love,

Maria

Becoming Unstoppable

From the QUEEN of getting back up...
Megan Ferrell

Who is Megan Ferrell?

A lady who wears many hats. Literally... Megan is the founder of Unstoppable/Unstoppable Women, living by the saying "Leave people better than you found them." Unstoppable was officially launched in June 2021. It started with a podcast and movement of spreading positive stories of people who have struggled but are now doing some really big things. From there it has grown at a rapid pace, and Megan now coaches men and women on their image and brand. With over 10 years of marketing experience and helping some big names in the industry grow their brand, Megan has landed herself on stages sharing her tools and is even finishing her first book, *Judge Not*.

Megan also has launched the Unstoppable Women side of this platform that specializes in helping working single moms who cannot qualify for government assistance but, still need help by giving them a hand up with yearly Dress for Success Day, The Christmas Project (Night of Hope Concert), and Back to School Hauls. This action has opened up a community of strong women who want to see others win along the way with them. We have built a tribe of women from all walks of life helping each other win from the CEO to the cashier, and you better believe they all bring value to our table.

Instagram: Megan_615 VIP

TikTok: Megan_615VIP

Website: YouRunstoppable.com

Email: Megan@urunstoppable.com

———

As I sit here and look out at the Nashville skyline from my Dolly Parton themed airbnb I am staying at to write this piece for our book... I can't help but think about all the chapters in my life that led me to this place today and made me who I am.

Someone once said I am the queen of getting back up. I think about that a lot. What made me that way? Could it be almost seeing my dad die in front of me at age 15 from a racecar accident where he was in the ICU and rehab for three months? Could it be my many failed attempts at finding true love, some great relationships, and some very very bad ones that ended in heartbreak, some with years of trauma I had to work through? Could it be being the only woman on my mom's side of the family who has been divorced? Could it be picking up the pieces of my life in a small town and starting over? Could it be being a single parent most of my kids' lives and having to live paycheck to paycheck wondering when I will be able to make more, have more for them? (By the way my babies are so precious, and we make one hell of a team!) Could it be my youngest son's health battles he faced when he was little and having to be his full time caregiver for the first three years of his life, allowing me to only pick up some odds and ends jobs part time to make ends meet? Could it be learning to know my worth and see all the amazing qualities about myself despite my failures and shortcomings of always trying to be a people pleaser and having no personal boundaries?

The fact is it is ALL of that! If we don't go through the hard and the challenges and get back up, the hard wins. The naysayers win! My Granny Dean said a long time ago, "Megan we all live in glass houses. People need to be careful who throws rocks." That stuck out to me and allowed me to walk in grace and to walk in my calling. It allowed me to meet the man of my dreams who loves me and babies so well! It allowed me to be fearless when it came to achieving my dreams. It allowed me to know what was real and what was fake. It allowed me to know what healthy personal boundaries look like and when someone is using me. It allowed me to know what grace is and how to walk in it. It allowed me to be authentically Megan.

The truth is life is hard for everyone. Some people are just packaged differently. My life came with a lot of falling down and getting back up, but the key to where I'm at today is that I didn't stay there, and I got back up. I took the lessons that life threw at me, and I learned from them and became a better person. The truth is I've always been a great person, even though others, and even myself, have said otherwise sometimes.

When I started Unstoppable, I took years and years of failure and hard times and put together a platform to help other women achieve greatness to find their worth, their voice, and to know that they always have a seat at our table. I also started with helping single moms who can't get assistance because they make too much money but still need help. A lot of these moms suffer in silence, never asking for help because they are afraid of being judged like they have been so many times. I was that mom, and having this platform now and seeing moms have help with Christmas, or a new wardrobe, or kids' school supplies makes my heart so very full.

Going through what I went through made me stronger, tougher, and more compassionate than I ever could have dreamed. What started out as being a movement to empower women has also trickled over to men. Unstoppable is a movement for everyone; it's about getting up and starting over. It's about not staying down. It's about being there for your fellow brother or sister! It's about not judging each other for our faults, but helping each other see the good and the power that lies within each other. It's about being able to leave the room and know you're not going to be talked about badly, only good! It's truly empowering because those who are at our table have walked through the hard and have come through it and are now helping others along the way.

It's truly about being UNSTOPPABLE!!

When I was asked to be a part of this series. I was honored, and I thought, *I have so much to write about.* Where do I start? My main story is going to be saved for my own book, *Judge Not,* that I'm working on because it's too many words, and I'm limited to my words with this one, but I want to leave you the reader with affirmations, the power of not quitting on yourself, the power of not waiting on someone else to give you permission to live your life, and the power to do something or go after your dream that you've been wanting to do. Stop worrying about what other people think; stop worrying about what if. Stop worrying about whether you are qualified. You need to start seeing yourself as a version that you want to be and that you know you're destined to be.

You need to forgive yourself for things that have happened that are out of your control, even some that were *in* your control. You need to remember why you started and why you were doing what you're doing by saying *yes* to your calling. By not quitting and being Unstoppable, you are helping a new generation come into their voice and come into their calling, my friend. If you take anything from this piece, I pray it's to know that you are truly fearfully and wonderfully made. And no matter what has been or will be thrown at you, you are ready, and YOU WILL succeed! Keep your light shining bright and always always be UNSTOPPABLE!

A New Season

Kimberly Greenwell

Kimberly Greenwell, a seasoned home expert, realtor, and host of the acclaimed TV show *My Southern Home*, blends her unparalleled media expertise with a passion for bringing aspirational homes to life. Kimberly offers valuable insights on renovation and homebuilding, guiding viewers through the process and connecting them with trusted professionals such as architects, contractors, realtors, and interior designers.

Kimberly's media journey began at Eastern Kentucky University, where she earned her degree in Broadcasting. She then launched her career at WAVE 3 as an advertising account executive, where she worked for seven years. Her experience there, combined with her role at Borrell Associates, where she collaborated with media outlets across the country, equipped her with a comprehensive expertise in both interactive and traditional media.

In 2009, Kimberly founded KAG Media Consulting, LLC. Her enthusiasm for home building and remodeling intensified while managing public relations for the Building Industry Association (BIA) of Greater Louisville's home-related events. This experience paved the way for her hosting role on *Your Kentuckiana Home,* and in 2017, she launched her own show, *My Southern Home with Kimberly Greenwell,* which quickly expanded to Nashville, Tenn., just a year later.

In January, Kimberly earned her real estate license and joined Crye-Leike, Realtors. This new role enables her to not only assist her viewers in designing their dream homes through her television show but also help them find the perfect property.

Kimberly relocated to Brentwood, Tenn., last year and is fully immersed in the Middle Tennessee community, embracing its Southern charm and the abundant opportunities it offers.

Instagram: @mysouthernhometv

Facebook: @mysouthernhometv

Kimberly@mysouthernhometv.com

———

I have always loved the word "new." It is a beautiful feeling. The word "new" covers an array of meanings, from items you can physically touch to feelings or experiences that bring intense happiness or overflowing emotions. A bright shiny new red car, a sparkling emerald and diamond necklace, or a feeling of renewal as you transition into a new season of life.

This is why spring has always been my favorite season. The bitter, harsh cold weather gives way to the soft, warm spring air. Easter flowers and tulips stir underneath the ground slowly, growing stronger, rising up, and pushing through the earth's surface to grace us with their vibrant colors and the feeling of hope that longer, brighter days are around the corner and a new season of life is on its way.

This past year has been a new season of life for me. I received the rare and beautiful opportunity to refresh, recharge, and create a new chapter filled with a sense of community, using my skills and network to help those in need and create a new career that brings me immense joy!

My work—the title associated with my name—has always been my identity. As someone who loves to work and has always loved what I do, the two come hand in hand. In 2009, I lost my father and was laid off from a glamorous job of flying all over the country and working with television stations, while I was running for a seat in the Kentucky state legislature.

Once the votes were cast—with not enough in my favor—and the campaign ended, I had to finally face dealing with my father's death, the loss of my job, and the big decision of what was next in life. Like all great creative entrepreneurs, I decided an economic downturn was the perfect time to start my own business. Just like that, a new season of life began, and KAG Media Consulting, LLC, was born.

Like all things in life, God had a greater plan and had already weaved my future together; I just didn't know it yet.

Running for office, my long career in media, and my relationships in the community gave way to my first contract with the Home Builders Association of Greater Louisville, now known as the Building Industry Association of Greater Louisville. They hired me to grow awareness and sponsorship sales for their consumer home-related events.

I didn't know it at the time, but this single opportunity would grow into a life that I couldn't image having for myself and a dream long forgotten: being in front of the camera. As a small-town girl growing up in Bardstown, Ky., I loved the camera. I modeled, competed in pageants, and set foot on Eastern Kentucky University's beautiful campus with one goal: being the next Diane Sawyer.

During college, I started taking voice lessons and was dedicated to rising above the pack and making my mark in broadcast television. Fate turned its head once again in my life. My advisor, knowing that I had competed nationally in marketing competitions in high school, thought that I should consider media sales. Being a sponge who was open to all things in the media world, I applied for a job as an account executive for our school newspaper, *The Eastern Progress*.

It was my first real interview. I remember walking into the office. I was a mixture of emotions: scared, excited, and apprehensive, while at the same time being internally fierce, telling myself that I was the best person for the job; it was mine for the taking.

After class the next day, I was greeted with a flashing red button on the answering machine. I hit play and jumped for joy when I heard the four words, *"Eastern Progress,"* and "you're hired!"

The energy of the sales office and the newsroom together was exhilarating for me. The hum of the computers, the smell of the wax, the late-night deadlines, the excitement of holding a fresh new paper in your hands, and seeing your hard work in black and white—it was beautiful, and I loved it.

Even with the allure of seeing my work in print, the bright lights and faster pace of television were calling my name. It would become one of my true loves. By the time I graduated from Eastern Kentucky University, I had been working in media sales for three years.

I had job offers all over the country, I decided to take one closer to home and settled in Louisville, Ky. The small-town girl finally made it to the big city, and I was ready for big things. Like all things in your life, when you soar toward the moon, you land in the stars.

In November 2000, I received the opportunity of a lifetime: an interview at WAVE 3-TV, the local NBC affiliate. Every Friday night in high school, we would hear the sound of their bright red helicopter flying in to cover the Nelson County Cardinals football game. My friends and I would race home after the game, hoping to catch a glimpse of ourselves in the background.

WAVE was our station. We watched the trusted anchors and meteorologists every day, and NBC was must-see TV every Thursday night! *Seinfeld*, *ER*, and *Friends* were the hottest shows in the country.

This little girl from Bardstown, who wanted to see herself on TV during WAVE 3's *Friday Night Flights* coverage, was now walking through their glass doors on the corner of Floyd and Broadway for an interview that was about to change her life. Once again, I came home to a flashing red button on the answering machine to hear those gorgeous four words: "WAVE 3," and "you're hired!"

Just like the Easter flowers and tulips bursting through the earth's surface, life has many twists and turns before the green stem develops into a magnificent flower. The life lessons you learn along the way and the jobs you land are layers of fertilizer nurturing you, making you stronger, and giving you the tools to grow into your purpose.

We all have a purpose, just like the wind. It whispers to you every day if you are open and pay attention. I am so thankful it found me.

Fast forward to 2015, I was at the corner of Shelbyville Road and Hurstbourne Lane. It was a brutal, cold December day. Big, fluffy snowflakes were falling all around me. It was another moment in my life that I will never forget.

I answered the phone to find out my life was about to come full circle; life's twists and turns had brought me back to television, and this time, in front of the camera. On that snowy

December day, I picked up the phone to an opportunity that would intertwine my two loves: beautiful homes and broadcast television.

Working with the home builders, I discovered something about myself that I didn't know: a love of all things home! This was the first time I had ever worked in the building industry. One of the big events I promoted for the local home builders association was Homearama, a single-site tour of homes that boasted the latest and greatest in new construction and design.

When I got out of my car and walked through the gates of the development for the first time, the same feeling I had when I walked into *Eastern Progress* rushed over me, but this time, it was from the smell of lumber, the roar of heavy equipment, the pounding of hammers, and the buzz of power tools creating homes.

On April 25th, my birthday, the first episode of *Your Kentuckiana Home* aired. Television wasn't new to me, but hosting and producing it was. Just like the wide-eyed freshmen at Eastern Kentucky University, I threw myself into learning everything I could. I hired a voice and acting coach and critiqued every episode, getting better and better each season.

Eventually, I found myself at a crossroads. No matter how hard I tried, the show was never what I envisioned, and my hands were tied. I didn't own the show and had no control over the end product.

In April 2017, I was in Nashville celebrating my 40th birthday, running the St. Jude Rock n' Roll marathon. During the trip, I shared my frustration with one of my friends. He said something to me that would be a pivotal moment in my life: "Start your own show."

I thought he was crazy! How could I start my own television show? After many long discussions and sleepless nights, I realized that I had every skill needed to start a television show. I was the executive producer, account executive, and host of a television show, plus I knew all the key players in the home industry.

In May of 2017, I came up with the name, created a logo, created a media kit, and started selling. Within two weeks, I had the title sponsor, and the first two episodes sold. *My Southern Home with Kimberly Greenwell* was born.

I watched the first episode on my father's birthday, August 2nd, and it aired a few days later. That same week, Barber Cabinet Company asked me if I would consider expanding the show to Nashville, Tenn., and I said *yes*!

In 2017, I knew only two people in Nashville, so I joined the Home Builders Association of Middle Tennessee and started networking. I used my skills and training from WAVE 3 once again, this time to launch my show in a brand-new city and one of the hottest real estate markets in the country!

It took seven months, but I did it! In August of 2018, I launched *My Southern Home with Kimberly Greenwell* in Music City, USA. In another full circle moment, I launched my very own show in a city that I loved, where just one year ago, the idea was born. Still, to this day, that is hard to wrap my head around. It was a very exciting time in my life.

I was making new friends, exploring a new city, and expanding my skills and knowledge in television and the home industry. I was making my own little mark in the world, blending my two loves, and living a dream that I didn't even know I had: using my love of television to help people create and build their dream homes. How did I get so lucky?

What I didn't know was that as the show grew and the years passed, I was slowly creating my own version of the Charles Dickens novel, *The Tale of Two Cities*. The show had become so big, and I was doing everything. Instead of owning the show, the show was starting to own me and was beginning to feel like my own little prison.

I was slowly dying inside and didn't even really know it. As glamorous as my life looked, it was very lonely. I was living a very transient life: going from city to city, always working, juggling four television shows at one point, and trying to figure out how to be in two places simultaneously.

My schedule was constantly changing on a dime. Friends would ask me to join them at events and parties, and I could never really commit. My life had become a checkerboard, and I was losing the game.

I didn't know it then, but I longed to be grounded, have a sense of community, and be still.

I always say that the universe whispers, yells at you, and then pushes you down. In 2023, I had that moment. I was breaking, and something needed to change; I didn't know what.

I was at another crossroads, but I didn't know what to do. I loved my show; I had worked so hard to create it, and we were making a difference. Every Saturday and Sunday in Kentucky and Tennessee, I helped people with their homes, but I also knew something had to give.

Like that fateful day in 2017, another friend gave me the answer I had been praying for. "Have you ever thought about getting your real estate license and marrying it with your show?"

I didn't need to give up the show; I needed to downsize to one market! It was brilliant. I had my answer; now, I just needed to be brave enough to do it.

Unlike before, I took several months to act on my new plan. It was hard; I had just renovated my condo, it was gorgeous, and I had hand-picked every piece. I finally had the dream space I encouraged my viewers to have.

I had lived in Louisville for over 20 years; it is where everything began, but really if you think about it, it started in Nashville.

I knew in my heart that my future was in Nashville. The energy and the people filled my soul like a moth to a flame. It wasn't an easy decision, but rather a long road with many prayers and conversations with people I love and respect, who helped me grow the show.

It was time to take my life back and start building a new future. Just like starting the show in 2017, once I made the decision, it was full steam ahead, and I didn't look back. I put my house on the market, got a place in Nashville, and started the process of closing down the Louisville market.

I worked during the day and went to real estate school at night, passing my test on January 2nd, two days into the new year. "New," that lovely word: I was about to have a new life, filled with new opportunities. The longing to be grounded, to be still, and to have a community was almost in my grasp.

It has been almost a full year since I decided to close down the show in Louisville. Much like when I started the show, some people thought I was crazy to do this; it would be like taking a step back.

Like before, when people thought the show would fail, I proved them wrong! It took me over a year to close down the Louisville market and wrap up my obligations. Like spring flowers, the best things about a new season take time.

Now, the show is better than ever. I had my first closing and my first listing and came back full circle, back to my roots, launching my own Tour of Homes. For the first time in seven years, my life is steady and grounded, and even though I still move at a fast pace, I have a sense of peace that I am where I need to be.

Like flowers, we all need to be in one place for our roots to grow strong, push through the surface, and embrace our full potential. I'm not afraid anymore to give myself water, sunlight, and the nourishment I need to be strong.

I'm not afraid to listen to the whispers and follow my heart. Life has shown me over and over to embrace the "new." New seasons, new places, and opportunities that are ours to grow into.

Embracing Creativity and Entrepreneurship

By Jennifer Moore

Jennifer Moore is a dedicated artist and entrepreneur in Nashville, Tenn., known for her innovative approach to custom finishes and mixed media art. Growing up in Louisiana, she was inspired by the rich local culture, which fueled her passion for the arts. After starting her career in the dynamic Nashville arts scene, she transitioned into creating textured, emotionally resonant art pieces. Jennifer also teaches and mentors aspiring artists and is actively involved in advocating for greater support and recognition of the arts in her community. Her work, influenced by nature and travel, aims to inspire and connect people through meaningful artistic expression.

www.wallstowalls.net
www.JenniferMoore.art
Instagram: @Wallstowallsstudio
Facebook: @wallstowalls

———

My journey into the world of art and entrepreneurship has been a tapestry woven with diverse experiences and profound personal growth, from the vibrant culture of Louisiana to the bustling streets of Nashville. As a child growing up in Louisiana, I was surrounded by the state's rich creative energy, and I found myself irresistibly drawn to the expressive arts. Music, sculptures, and the endless possibilities of the liberal arts captivated my imagination from an early age. My mother, a creative soul in her own right, nurtured my budding interests, creating spaces where my passion for fashion and design could flourish. We spent countless weekends picking out fabrics and crafting designs that reflected my evolving style, bonding over our shared love of creativity.

After high school and a brief stint in college, I set my sights on New York, eager to immerse myself in its artistic culture. However, a stop in Nashville, Tenn., altered my path. There, I found myself drawn to the dynamic music video scene, where I embraced every aspect of production—from set design to makeup artistry. These early experiences taught me the transformative power of designing spaces, a skill that would later define my entrepreneurial journey.

At 19, I became a solo parent, a profound turning point in my life. Balancing motherhood with work in the service industry, I juggled long shifts while nurturing my freelance projects in design and décor. Despite the challenges, I pursued my passion relentlessly, gradually expanding my skills into custom finishes, drapery work, and furniture restoration. Determined to deepen my artistic repertoire, I embarked on a journey to master faux finishing techniques, taking classes in Florida and North Carolina. These experiences provided me with the knowledge and confidence to transform my skills into a professional portfolio. Despite life's setbacks, I persevered, homeschooling my children while honing my craft in design and decorative finishes. Learning to listen to a client's desire to create personal spaces that reflect their personalities has been a gift. There is immense satisfaction in witnessing the delight on a client's face when a project is completed, knowing that I've successfully bridged their thoughts and reality.

One pivotal moment in my late 20s stands out as a turning point in how I viewed my life. I was chatting with a lady from my Bible study who was giving me a ride. As we talked, she asked about my life, and I shared openly, as I often did. I had a habit of being an open book, sometimes revealing more than I should.

That tendency often left me feeling exposed or ashamed afterward. But her response was different. Instead of reacting with pity or surprise, she simply said, "Your life is so colorful."

Those words meant the world to me. They changed how I viewed my past, my experiences, and my traumas. I began to see the richness and depth in my journey, rather than focusing solely on the pain. Today, I'm grateful that my work and passion bring color into my life, and I hope to continue bringing that same vibrancy to the lives of those around me.

As life's challenges continued to shape my path, I faced yet another crossroads following a divorce after 15 years of marriage. With an unfinished degree and a small designer painting business, I made the bold decision to fully commit to entrepreneurship. With limited resources, I embraced self-promotion and networking, leveraging face-to-face interactions to grow my clientele and forge lasting connections. Networking, particularly with like-minded professionals, taught me a life-changing lesson: We are not islands. We need a community where we can recharge, lift each other up, and offer encouragement. Investing in others provides the support we need to keep moving forward, even when fear threatens to derail our efforts.

Beyond transforming physical spaces, my art became a sanctuary for emotional expression. Experimenting with mixed media allowed me to explore themes of healing and connection more deeply. Moving beyond decorative finishes, I began creating textured, meaningful art pieces that resonate with personal stories and reflections. This evolution marked a pivotal moment in my creative journey, as I discovered a new dimension to my artistry—one that I eagerly share with others.

Seeking to reach beyond my local community, I began teaching and mentoring aspiring artists, which became a fulfilling part of my journey. I taught workshops and classes in my Nashville studio, sharing my knowledge and passion for art and creativity with others. My teaching philosophy centers on encouraging individual expression and creativity. I believe that every artist has a unique voice, and my role as a teacher is to help students find and develop that voice. Nurturing and supportive, I create a positive and inclusive learning environment, a skill I honed while homeschooling my children. As a result, many of my students have gone on to pursue successful careers in decorative painting and the arts.

My belief in the power of art to heal and connect people extends beyond my personal work and teaching. I am actively involved in community business groups, where I bring simple business practices to aspiring entrepreneurs and creators. I advocate for greater support and recognition for the arts, working with local art organizations to secure funding and resources, and promoting the importance of art in education and community development. I serve on the board of the Williamson County Cultural Arts Commission, the Tennessee International Indie Film Festival, and the International Decorative Artisan League.

Outside of my professional life, I find inspiration in the world around me. I enjoy spending time in nature, where I often find ideas for my work in the colors, patterns, and textures of the natural world. These elements are a constant source of inspiration, influencing my use of color and form. I also find joy in traveling, exploring different cultures and artistic traditions, which enrich my work by adding layers of meaning and context. Collaborating with fellow artists and creatives further expands my artistic horizons, leading to new and exciting projects.

My journey through entrepreneurship and creativity has been defined by resilience, passion, and a steadfast belief in the transformative power of art. From humble beginnings in Louisiana to navigating the challenges of solo parenthood and career setbacks, each experience has shaped me into the artist and entrepreneur I am today. Through it all, I've learned the importance of adapting to change, embracing challenges as opportunities for growth, and staying true to my artistic vision.

As I continue to evolve professionally and personally, I remain committed to using my talents not only to beautify spaces but also to inspire and empower others on their own creative journeys. I hope that my journey serves as a testament to my passion, resilience, and commitment to my craft. Through my art, I aim to create beautiful and meaningful pieces that inspire and connect people. My journey is a reminder of the power of creativity and the importance of staying true to one's vision. As I continue to evolve as an artist, I remain dedicated to making a positive impact with my art and leaving a lasting legacy for future generations. For me, art isn't just about aesthetics—it's about storytelling, healing, and creating meaningful connections that transcend the physical realm. In every stroke of paint and design decision, I find fulfillment knowing that I'm making a positive impact, one space—and one life—at a time.

My Fight Song

Hannah Noel

Hannah Noel is striking the hearts of dreamers everywhere one song at a time. This Southeast Georgia native began playing the guitar at the ripe age of six and writing songs on her childhood playroom floor at 12. Hannah graduated from Belmont University's highly acclaimed Songwriting Program and was the recipient of the 2020 ASCAP (American Society of Composers, Authors and Publishers) Foundation Bart Howard Scholarship Award.

Noel's unique sound has been compared to Sugarland, Reba McEntire, Lainey Wilson, and many more. Throughout her years of performing, she has played Muscle Shoals Songwriters Festival, Fernandina Beach Songwriters Festival, Universal Music Group's Malibu Cook-off, The Listening Room, Whiskey Jam, 3rd and Lindsley, Mockingbird Theater, and many more venues and festivals.

Recently, Hannah Noel was named part of *Today's Country Magazine's* Class of 2023, which describes her sound as "a moody blend of honky-tonk rhythm, modern country edge, and a touch of spitfire."

The budding star's recent single, "Don't Sell Your Saddle," went to country radio in 2023, spreading a strong message of encouragement through her powerhouse vocals and lush lyricism. Performing at the largest CMA award-winning terrestrial radio stations such as 94.7 The Country Giant and US 101 (WUSY-FM), Hannah Noel is named an up-and-coming country artist to watch.

Website: www.hannahnoelmusic.com
Instagram: @hannahnoelmusic
Facebook: @hannahnoelmusic

———

With pride and bloody fingertips, I ran to my dad after countless hours of practice on my playroom floor. For years he would tell me to play the guitar until my fingers bled, creating calluses worn by the most dedicated guitarists. I remember him responding to my joy with, "Good! Now go play some more."

My guitar has truly seen blood, sweat, and tears. Conjoined to my hip, it holds the secrets of a child who snuck too many candies and the burdens of a now 23-year-old woman. It's had the closest look at my broken heart, and helped mend it back together. It's heard lyrics that will never see the light of day. It was there for me when I had no friends, and it was there when I had many. It's sung joyful tunes of make-believe and of gut-wrenching truths.

Sometimes I think my guitar might be the death of me—and truthfully, I'd let it.

My father started teaching me to play when I was six years old; to this day, he is the only teacher I have ever had. In the first grade, I put on my first-ever performance for my class' show and tell. My dad never found out until I walked through my front door from school that day with my guitar in my hand and my mom carrying my amp. He still gives me heck for not being able to say he was at my first performance. Truthfully, I thought nothing of it at the time. All I knew was one simple fact: my duty was to put on a show.

I have no memories of playing with dolls, but I have plenty of memories of stealing the fog machine out of the storage closet, dressing up my younger brother and sister, and performing whatever songs I had forced them into listening to that day. From a young age, I knew I was put on this earth to write songs, play them for people, and entertain. More than that, I have always longed for human connection, relation, and storytelling. I still have that strong assurance that music is my calling, and without it, I know I would not have made it as far as I have.

I remember being 14 and staying home all summer to practice. I had begged my parents to homeschool me through high school so that I could spend more time developing my musical talents. I spent the entire summer practicing, to the point that my parents were becoming concerned about why I was choosing to stay home all the time. That was when it clicked for them: I really *was* as dedicated as I led on. There was no denying my skills as they had improved dramatically.

That fall, I began homeschool. I didn't care one bit about being in a classroom with kids my own age, calling myself a part of a sports team, or anything that high school normalcy entailed. All I cared about was practicing and performing. I knew that to not only be great, but be one of the greats, required sacrifice, but it didn't feel like sacrifice at the time. My weekends were spent playing three-hour sets with my dad who had quickly become my sound guy, roadie, and "dadager." All I longed for was this time with him, being on the road, and an audience.

At 19, I recorded my first record in Nashville at Ocean Way Studios just before finally making the big move to Music City. Everyone expected the awkward homeschooler to have a hard time leaving home, but that couldn't have been further from the truth. I was finally surrounded by people who shared the same irrational love for music that I did. There's a sense of community in Nashville that I have found surprises most people. Don't get me wrong, you will find your fair share of Broadway cowboys who are all hat and no cattle, but there's not much tinsel in this town. I have found that most people are the real deal and deserve their dreams just as much as I do.

I remember the feeling in my chest clearly, the one I got during my first visit to Nashville. It was almost euphoric—a stomach-sinking, spiritual experience. As a kid, I'd told my parents I belonged in Nashville. She had always called me, and I had to chase her back. The certainty of that moment alone gave me hope for my career and legacy as an artist. After that moment, I always found a way back.

I bring these few monumental moments in my life to you in an effort to highlight the bittersweet edge of having a dream and the suffering it entails, but when you want it bad enough, it's all counted as fuel and, on good days, joy.

Today, I write this with an abundance of joy, as it is the first time in weeks I have been able to move my hands with minimal pain.

While I sacrificed being with family during major life events for shows at dives and morning co-writing sessions, what most don't know is that I was also battling an illness. I am currently in the late stages of chronic Lyme disease. As a child, I was bitten by a tick that caused me to become increasingly ill, and I did not find out the cause until now, 2024.

I remember the first show I ever played with a high-grade fever, and praying between songs that God would keep me upright while I was on stage. Playing my small-town Western bar with a 102-degree fever was not supposed to be in the cards.

Slaying Nashville

I never let a soul there know that I was anything less than the blonde-haired, starry-eyed performer that they hired, because the show must always go on. This mentality was ingrained into my soul at a young age, and I know it will stick with me forever.

Being sick made life harder in the expected ways, but also in the aspects of creating. It has never stopped me though. I think the largest obstacle for most is just showing up. If I show up, the song always does too.

There are plenty of artists all around town, just like me, who deserve country music to love them back, but are still waiting for the day. We have all played countless four-hour gigs to crowded rooms, and even more shows to empty bars. We've all ripped our hearts out and put them in songs, only to find that the bartenders were the only ones listening. We all write hundreds of songs that will never be heard. We even forget some of the songs ourselves because we are constantly onto the next idea that could be our ticket to the big leagues. Some joke and say it's all just a big noodle-eating contest to see who can live off of ramen the longest, because it's a big waiting game.

I've found that keeping my head down and putting in the work is the best course of action, because as soon as you start playing the comparison game to another artist's journey, your journey begins to slow down—and no one in this town can afford to do that. I've been through hell and back pursuing this dream, so much so that I wonder if my drive to not give up is born of pure stubbornness. However, I believe some of the greatest women to grace this earth are stubborn as hell. It all comes back to knowing in my heart that music is my calling. Deep down, I know artistry is the only path I could take that will ever see true success because I know that God's hand is in it... and why go where God's hand is not?

During this time of healing, I've come to the conclusion that it's not about who is the most talented, but about who works the hardest. What do you do when you feel you have worked as hard as you can? You keep on. In Nashville, you must find a way to be louder in the midst of a bunch of noise.

However, something no one has ever told me in this town but something I have come to rely on greatly (especially in my current condition) is that some of the greatest things in life find their way to you. I understand this feels quite contradictory to my "'nose-to-the-grindstone" attitude, but what about when you have worked so hard for so long, made sacrifice after sacrifice, and you can't help but let your humanity creep in? What happens when you stop and wonder, "What the heck am I even doing?"

What I have found is I'm not only chasing and striving, but I'm building the life, and the girl, I have always wanted to be. I say this in gained wisdom, not brutality; as a musician, you must never take *no* for an answer.

You must try your best to be happy for the young, fresh-off-the-bus, overnight success but also try not to pay too much attention to the clock, because this is a ten-year town.

Slaying Nashville

So why do it? Because when you're an artist, your heartbeat is a kickdrum, and you've gotta kick down every door just so it can keep beating.

Write Your Own Rules

Laura Pasyanos

Laura is the founder and owner of Southern Doula Services, where she combines her extensive knowledge and passion for maternal and newborn health to offer compassionate, personalized care. As a dedicated doula and agency owner, Laura ensures that families receive the support they need during one of life's most special and transformative moments. Her expertise is backed by her experience as a mother of four adult children, allowing her to deeply understand the joys and challenges of parenting. Family is at the core of everything Laura does, and she brings that same warmth and dedication to her doula work and to the families she serves through her agency. When she is not supporting families, she enjoys traveling with her family, especially if a beach is involved.

https://southerndoulaservices.com

www.instagram.com/southerndoulaservices.com

————

Life does not always go as planned, but sometimes unexpected detours lead to the most rewarding destinations.

My story begins in a small New England town where dreams were big and resources were limited. I was the first in my family to pursue a college education. Packed with the essentials and a whole lot of ambition, I was on my way to fulfilling my dreams by heading off to school.

At the start of my second semester, I found myself staring at a positive pregnancy test, grappling with the reality of becoming a teen mom. The whirlwind of emotions—from fear and uncertainty to a fierce sense of determination—set the stage for my life's journey. Little did I know that this unexpected turn of events would ignite a profound realization within me: the power to write my own story, regardless of the circumstances.

From the onset, I knew that education would be my lifeline. Growing up in a family that valued education, I was determined not to let the circumstances derail my dreams. Balancing college and motherhood was challenging, but I was resolute in my commitment. I was surrounded by a circle of support including my family, my boyfriend (now husband), and my college advisor and professors. Through it all, I was writing my own narrative, one where I refused to be defined by statistics or stereotypes.

Fast-forward a few years, and I was married to my high school sweetheart. Our little family of three quickly grew to a family of six in just a few short years. I was that mom with four children, ages five and under. Yes, I was that "crazy" lady you see pushing the double stroller, with a baby on her hip and another child holding on; these were some of my happiest memories. I got to grow up alongside my children, and they became my biggest motivators. My two oldest were at my college graduation when I graduated *summa cum laude* with an education degree. I was living proof that you could define your life, not by your circumstances, but by your choices and actions. My children watched me struggle and triumph, learning the values of resilience and hard work firsthand.

Entering the classroom as a kindergarten teacher was a dream come true. For 15 years, I poured my heart into teaching, creating a nurturing environment where my students could thrive. It also allowed me to be the kind of mom I wanted to be, having summers and school vacations off to enjoy my children. Each day was a new adventure, filled with laughter and curiosity. I took pride in knowing I was laying the foundation for my students' future successes, just as I was doing for my own children at home.

Then life got flipped upside-down when my husband was offered a promotion with a relocation to Tennessee. A very far reach out of my comfort zone and over a thousand miles away from the place I called home for over 40 years. As much as I loved teaching, I also couldn't ignore the growing feeling that it was time for a change. New address, new state, new career. My story was calling for a new chapter.

Around this time, my family had been approved for foster care, a calling that sat on my heart for years and finally came to fruition. We specialized in infant placements. The juxtaposition of raising teenagers while welcoming infants to the household was profound. It was a clear reminder to me just how much I enjoyed the newborn stage of life—perhaps one of the reasons why I have four children. It was this realization that would ultimately shape my next career move. To be very honest, when I first heard about doula work, I thought it was mainly supporting births, but as soon as I found out about postpartum doula care I realized that my skills as an educator and as a mother could be channeled into helping new families navigate the postpartum period. The transition from teaching to becoming a postpartum doula felt like a natural progression, allowing me to continue nurturing and supporting others but in a different capacity.

Once again, I was redefining my path centered on my heart to serve, and ultimately crafting a narrative that aligned with my passions and strengths.

Starting my journey as a postpartum doula, I immersed myself in the training and certification programs, eager to provide the best care possible. I was fortunate enough to have a supportive network of friends and family who believed in my vision. The work was deeply gratifying, and I found immense joy in helping families transition into parenthood with confidence and ease. My story was becoming one of service and empowerment, helping others find strength during vulnerable times. That training led some of my own emotions to resurface that I had never quite addressed. These emotions are part of a mental health issue that is quite honestly not talked about enough: postpartum mood and anxiety disorder (PMAD).

My oldest daughter was born two months premature, which brought on a whole level of emotions. I was so hyper-focused on her well-being that my mental health took a backseat. We were fortunate in so many ways from the expert-level medical care we received to the fighting spirit of my itty bitty three-pound baby. She was strong and healthy, and by the time she was 12 months old, you would not have even known she was a preemie. I was immersed in motherhood, balancing work and school to finish my degree, and had my eye on the prize the whole time. When I found myself pregnant two-and-a-half years later, I was so eager to be solely focused on my family.

So my expectations were that this was going to be a smooth transition for me. The opposite was true. I ended up with severe, debilitating anxiety after the birth of my son. It seems so silly to put into words but I had this overwhelming sense of dread and worry that something would happen to me and no one would be able to raise my babies the way I knew I would. In my mind, the most dangerous place to be was in a car, so I literally stopped driving. I went to doctor's appointments and all the essential errands and... *That. Was. It.* The thought of being in the car for any length of time would bring on severe panic attacks. And the entire thing was so irrational that I kept it to myself.

Statistics say one in five women experience some type of PMAD; however, I believe it to be closer to one in three. I believe this because I know there are plenty of others like me who suffer in silence.

I was more determined than ever to rewrite the narrative for postpartum moms, derail society's expectations, and truly hold space for new moms as they start this chapter of their lives. As my reputation grew, so did my ambition. I realized the significant demand for postpartum support, and I wanted to make a broader impact. With a blend of trepidation and excitement, I decided to launch my own doula agency. My goal was to create a team of doulas who could provide exceptional care to families during one of the most vulnerable times in their lives. I was not only writing my story, but I was also helping others write theirs.

Running a new business was a whole new challenge, but my journey had prepared me well. The resilience and resourcefulness I had cultivated as a teen mom and educator proved invaluable. I navigated the complexities of entrepreneurship, from marketing and client management to financial planning and team building. Each success, no matter how small, was a testament to the power of perseverance and passion. I was determined to show my children and my community that it is possible to define your life on your terms, no matter where you start.

Today my agency is thriving, and I am proud to say that we have supported countless families through their birth and postpartum journeys. We have grown into a six-figure business, but more importantly, we have made a real difference in the lives of the families we serve. As I look to the future, I am excited about the possibilities. I plan to expand my agency, focusing on the informational and educational needs of our families, advocating for overall better postpartum support, and mentoring the next generation of doulas.

My journey is a testament to the fact that, no matter where you start, with determination and perseverance, you can achieve your dreams. As an 18-year-old facing the daunting reality of teenage motherhood, I found myself at a crossroads, surrounded by societal expectations and doubts. Yet, within the chaos, I discovered a profound truth: the power to write my own rules.

This became the guiding force of my journey, propelling me through the challenges of raising four children, pursuing a career in education, and ultimately transforming my life to become a successful entrepreneur. And the ink on this chapter is still wet as I continue to write the next pages. Stay tuned...

Success = My Tennessee Dream Home on the Lake

Serena Sacks-Mandel

Ms. Sacks-Mandel is an international award-winning strategic visionary and sales and operations leader. She recently joined MGT as the field CTO supporting Social Impact Solutions and Technology Solutions Group. In her previous roles, she was the global chief technology officer at Microsoft for the education industry and the chief information officer at Fulton County Schools and Florida Virtual Schools. In both organizations she led the IT function to become "world-class," while enabling student-centric teaching and learning, which resulted in significant improvements in student outcomes.

Prior to pivoting to education, she led technology innovation teams at IBM, Walt Disney World, and Harcourt, Inc., and provided management consulting support for many other organizations. Ms. Sacks-Mandel has won numerous state, national, and global awards for her leadership, vision, technical excellence, and commitment to supporting women in technology. She recently published her book ***Empowered***: ***Frame your Narrative, Own your Power***.

Connect with Serena at www.SerenaSacksMandel.com.

———

I have always been more of a lake and mountain person than a beach lover. What about you? When I met my husband five years ago, I fell in love not only with him, but with the Tennessee River, where he had a vacation lake house. The "lake" is eighty miles long with many inlets and large coves, which are often four miles wide. We are both more at peace and in a joyful state from the moment we arrive.

During the pandemic, while working there remotely, we decided to build our "forever home" in this paradise. Shortly after we were married, we found the perfect mountain-side deep-water lakefront property with diverse fauna and flora. Our current home is only four miles away, so we are able to stay deeply involved in the construction, which is taking a very long time. We are looking forward to moving in next spring.

We enjoy nature's beauty, peace, and fun every day. Whether we are boating, skiing, or just gazing at the water, trees, and birds, I feel grateful for the lake lifestyle. The lake is not the only thing I love about Tennessee. This state is full of wonders and surprises. We often visit Nashville, Knoxville, and Chattanooga and explore the natural and cultural diversity, from the majestic Smokey Mountains to the charming restaurants. We love white water rafting on the Ocoee River, two-stepping in Nashville, going to the big Vols game in Knoxville, hiking Piney River Falls, and visiting the attractions in Gatlinburg. Not to mention the fantastic distilleries and craft beer gastropubs!

Locally we see amazing wildlife, such as bald eagles, red foxes, osprey, hawks, and bass. We love picking up farm fresh eggs and produce. We could do without the spiders though; my husband takes care of them!

After overcoming a lifetime of challenges and obstacles, the respite on the water in Tennessee is oh so welcome and deserved! This is what I have worked for, to enjoy the rest of my life on the water and in my perfect home, which we only dreamed of for almost 60 years. This proves we can have it all, but maybe not all at the same time!

My professional career spans over 35 years in technology in consulting, sales, and leadership in several Fortune 500 companies, the public sector, and social impact organizations. I have been a professional speaker on leadership, culture, technology, and education for more than 25 years. Throughout this time, I have volunteered on healthcare, museum, and technology association boards too. All of this is what my LinkedIn profile shows, but it does not begin to tell my personal story of resilience, purpose, and perseverance despite significant family and health challenges.

My original nuclear family was rife with strife and dysfunction. With an emotionally and physically abusive father and moody, depressed mother, I literally became an adult at six years old when I negotiated child support and healthcare payments with my father. My parents had zero ability to soothe my wounds or show compassion. My mother's mantra was "self-sufficiency," picking yourself up. She would say, "Stop crying, or I'll give you something to cry about," and if I didn't stop crying she would slap me hard across the face. I learned early that if you cry, you cry alone.

I survived the war zone that was my younger years by denying emotions or feelings and powering through. I focused on my education, playing sports, and planning my future. Ultimately, my strength came from the ability to forgive these two flawed individuals and claim my power to be my own person.

As an adult, I chose a partner who "checked all the boxes", but 20 years into the relationship, I realized that they were the wrong boxes. I married a man who looked the part (tall, handsome, blue eyes) and had the pedigree for family approval (Cornell grad, lawyer). But he was not emotionally or physically present for me and our family which included two daughters. It was confusing on some level: we had a wonderful home, friends, and financial comfort. From the outside, we were an ideal family. However, walking on eggshells to avoid upsetting him was overwhelmingly stressful. Eventually, I gathered my courage and walked away to begin living my own life, making decisions for myself, albeit as a single mother.

In the seven years I was single, living in Atlanta, I won multiple awards as the chief information officer for Women in Technology, and for turning failing students and schools around, using data to tailor education. I felt like this was my best life. But then the bottom fell out. As I entered pre-menopause, something was not right. Over three weeks, I saw many doctors who assured me it was *not* cancer. Then I endured many procedures, including multiple diagnostic surgeries, and additional biopsies that ultimately revealed I had a very rare and aggressive form of uterine cancer. I was told surgery would be sufficient but a light chemo treatment would give me certainty that it would not recur. Unfortunately after nearly six months, the cancer actually came back worse with metastasis to my lungs. I then endured extremely aggressive chemo for the next six months. All of this happened while I continued working as CIO and taking care of my mother who had moved from Asheville to be near me after her husband passed. She was in the middle stages of Alzheimer's. It would take another year of significant physical, emotional, and mental ailments before I felt my biggest challenges in life were over. One month later, I met my soulmate at a free concert in the park.

While we were getting to know each other, we excitedly talked about the "dream house" we each had in mind. We sent pictures to each other and were not surprised that they matched! Our energy was and is magical, and we knew the universe would help us deliver this gift to each other, especially after everything I had overcome!

We were lucky to find the perfect property with 350 feet of lakefront and build our dream home. It took a lot of hard work, patience, and creativity, but we did it! We designed and built a beautiful and comfortable home that reflects our personality and style. We have a huge three-tiered deck for the best in indoor/outdoor living, an ample-sized "clean" kitchen with a large "dirty" kitchen pantry for storage and countertop appliances.

But wait, there is more! Let me tell you about some of the features and details that make our home so special and unique. My husband is building a bar, wine cellar, and a secret door that leads to a special space for curious grandchildren. We have a game room with a pool table, a dart board, and three game-ready TVs, one near the hot tub. We also have a hot tub, fire pit, and a two-slip dock complete with tri-toon, wave runners, kayaks, and standup paddleboards. We have a guest room with a lake view; come visit! We love hosting our friends and family and sharing our lake paradise with them, a kindness I'm happy to extend.

This quote by poet Bianca Sparacino is very true in my life: The kindest people are not born that way, they are made. They are the ones that have experienced so much at the hands of life, they are the ones who have dug themselves out of the dark, who have fought to turn every loss into a lesson. The kindest people do not just exist—they choose to soften where circumstance has tried to harden them; they choose to believe in goodness, because they have seen firsthand why compassion is so necessary. They have seen firsthand why tenderness is so important in this world.[3]

I talk more about my journey in my book *Empowered. Frame your Narrative. Own your Power.* My ability to overcome so many adversities is an inspiring tale of resilience and determination.

Hopefully this story serves as a beacon of hope for others facing similar challenges, reminding us that with perseverance and a positive attitude, we can overcome any obstacle and achieve our dreams. My experiences and lessons learned along the way provide valuable insights and inspiration for anyone striving to build a successful and fulfilling life and enjoy success on one's own terms.

I'm thankful that my journey made me the kind and caring person that I am today. And that it led me to that lake in Tennessee, where I can enjoy a more peaceful period of my life.

---

[3] https://tinybuddha.com/fun-and-inspiring/the-kindest-people-are-not-born-that-way/

Behind the Successful Façade

Victoria 'Tori' Staggs

Tori is a dedicated and passionate architect and designer who prides herself on designing with purpose, grace, and authenticity. Known for her ambitious spirit, Tori has a proven track record of redefining boundaries and pursuing impeccable feats, like becoming the first student at the University of Tennessee to ever study abroad in the Middle East (Israel). Outside of work, she enjoys oil painting, culinary adventures with her husband, and serving as a faithful woman of Christ, which reflects a commitment to creativity and grace. With a strong belief in a diligent and honest work ethic, Tori continues to push herself to create beautiful and meaningful moments and designs that bring light and beauty to the lives around her. Her passions and curiosity can be summed up by one of her favorite quotes:

God left the world unfinished for man to work his skill upon. He left the electricity in the cloud, the oil in the earth. He left the rivers unbridged and the cities unbuilt. God gives us the challenge of raw materials, not the ease of finished things. He leaves the pictures unpainted and the music unsung and the problems unsolved, that we might know the joys and glories of creation. - Thomas S. Monson.

Today, she is embarking on a variety of new adventures and explorations that are sure to broaden her passions and outreach. Her ambition and resilience are a true testament to her determination to make the most of the precious life that God has gifted her.

Instagram: @torikaystaggs
Facebook: @ToriStaggs

———

Beautiful rolling hills adorned with wildflowers, ancestral lands cherished by families for generations, and neighbors who have known each other for lifetimes—this is the backdrop of my childhood. Some would call living in a small rural town idyllic and peaceful, and I would agree. For many years, I convinced myself that I did not belong there, believing I was destined for greater things. I wanted to explore the world, win impressive medals, and become someone who inspired the next generation with my intelligence and achievements. My obsession with academic and career achievements led me to sacrifice much of the fulfillment and joy of my young adult life. In my own eyes, I became the hero-turned-desperate villain in the grand adventure stories I used to adore as a child, and I feel as if now, finally, I am returning to my humble roots.

Those who currently know me may be shocked to know that as a child, I was quite timid and shy. I hardly spoke my mind and would spend most of my time with my nose dug in a book or out playing on my grandparent's farm with my little sister and cousins. My favorite books were ones of daring adventure and great acts of bravery, with an occasional whimsical escapade sprinkled in. I would daydream of going on these great adventures and becoming a damning show of power and grace all the while being afraid of the dark and the possible monsters that hid behind every tree and corner.

As I grew and matured into my teenage years, some of those fears started to melt away and new ones set in. As with every teenager, I became obsessed with how my peers viewed me, and I wanted to create an image for myself that I could be proud of. What better character to portray myself as than the ones I had read about for so many years? Bold, strong, outspoken, and accomplished. So, over my adolescent and young adult life, I crafted my personality and character to be exactly that. I reached out and pushed every academic boundary I could set my sights on because I was determined to break a glass ceiling in a way that my little town hadn't seen before. To my knowledge, I am the first (or one of very few) students from my high school to pursue a career in architecture. Of course, I applied to the Ivy Leagues and some of the other best private and public schools the country had to offer, and I was proud to tell anyone who would listen that I was accepted into each and every one of them. Eventually, I decided to attend the University of Tennessee to pursue an education in architecture and design. From there, the character I had crafted began to excel and fall apart at the same time.

To be bold, courageous, and strong is not only praiseworthy, but it is the societal picture of leadership and success. However, what really makes someone truly bold, courageous, and strong is the foundation on which those traits are built. Unfortunately, due to a lack of wisdom and experience, my foundation was built from some of the only feelings I really understood at the time: insecurity, timidness, and lack of self-worth. I had constructed a façade of accomplishment and pride, all the while feeling overwhelmed, stressed, and unworthy.

At university, I excelled in all my classes and extracurriculars. I obtained internships before most of my classmates, collected academic and performance scholarships, won design awards in outside design competitions, and even became the first student at the University of Tennessee (UT) to study abroad in the Middle East (Israel). To say I worked hard is an understatement. I studied and researched until sunrise more times than I can count just to stay one step ahead of everyone else. There was no stopping me when it came to breaking through a barrier that was set before me.

I was outgoing, confident, and thirsty for success and praise through any means I could obtain it. Again, to others and society, I was the perfect picture of a new generation of leadership and innovation, but inside, I was constantly pushing myself to mental exhaustion because the success and accomplishments I had obtained over the years never felt "good enough." I was constantly searching for something bigger and better, more impressive even. I had come to realize that I was working toward creating a life and career that others would be jealous of or impressed by, rather than working and living to create a life that I truly enjoyed and felt proud of. My insecurities had created an existence of arrogance, self-loathing, and detrimental perfectionism all hidden behind an image of confidence and strength. The foundation of my success was cracked, and I didn't even realize it. I thought that this was how it was supposed to be.

My perspective started shifting when I decided to study abroad in Israel. I had created the program myself at UT, and to my understanding, I am the very first to do so. I spent months petitioning the United States government and the University of Tennessee regulators to obtain permission to study in the

Middle East. After that, I developed a program with a school that not only accepted a rogue student to study with them, but also provided the academic rigor required by UT to count toward my degree. After months of communication, documents, and meetings, I had achieved my goal of attending one of the top architecture schools in the world in northern Israel. However, the catch was, I was going completely by myself. I didn't know the language, had never been on a plane before, knew absolutely no one, and had no assistance navigating the country when I first arrived. I loved it.

I was able to become a completely different person and meet a variety of people from all over the world. I traveled all of Israel and took some daring adventures in the West Bank and Jordan. I met people from all sorts of backgrounds, and when appropriate, they let me see and experience life with them. From traveling nomads to humble shop owners and the occasional wandering local, every person I met added a layer of depth to my ever-evolving outlook on what it means to have a life and character that you can truly be proud of. Surprisingly enough, most of the people I met hadn't won some kind of impressive award or landed a high-paying, cushiony job (some were quite impoverished); yet, they were so grateful just to experience the day and whatever joys it brought. During my time there, I was attending class, but everything was so new that I was forced to focus on learning and adapting and exploring—so much so that I didn't have time to obsess over my own ideas of "success" and "power." On the plane ride home, I realized that the six months

I'd just spent abroad were like the adventure stories I adored so much when I was a child. My days were spent trying new things, stepping out of my comfort zone, being kind and generous with my time and experiences, and just enjoying the days for what they were. From then on, I knew something needed to change.

Over the past few years, I have been slowly crafting new adventures and completing different chapters in my life with a new definition of purpose and success. I have traded arrogance with grace, and people-pleasing with gratitude and generosity. I sometimes still fall into my old ways, yet the immense pressure of trying to achieve "perfection" or meet some goals of "success" seem to have shifted into experiences of humility and appreciation.

In the last five years, I started my career as an architect studying under one of the most talented architects in the region and got married to an amazing and genuine man who inspires me every day. I also planned and coordinated one of the largest, most popular, and wildly successful fundraising events in Nashville. I became a mother, and experienced many other new things, both professionally and personally. I am braver now than ever before because I am allowing myself to be vulnerable. I now focus less on the image I want to portray to the world, and allow my intentions to focus on connection, loyalty, and love for those I am blessed enough to interact with every day.

The purpose of this story is not to discourage anyone from setting out and achieving the impossible. In fact, I wholeheartedly encourage anyone to do so, and to do it fearlessly, without a hint of doubt. My hope is that you cultivate a genuine love for yourself, grounded in grace and self-worth, and build your confidence and courage on solid foundations, rather than what the world deems necessary for success.

A Legacy of Aloha through Entrepreneurship

Erin Takiue

Erin is a four-time salon owner, the CEO of Sanctuary Salon located in the West End area of Nashville, and a mom. Originally from Hawaii, she feels that bringing a "spirit of aloha" to Nashville is a special part of Sanctuary Salon.

Slaying Nashville

Website: Sanctuarysalonnashville.com

Instagram: @sanctuarysalonnashville

———

My family and I relocated from Hawaii to Nashville three years ago and purchased our third salon soon after. We currently work out of our fourth salon, which I built from the ground up! I am a mom of three children, ages 15, 12, and 8 and absolutely love being a hands-on mom who is busy with all their activities and sports. I have been a hairstylist for 22 years and a salon owner for 13 years.

My grandmother and grandfather helped fund and were the original supporters of the first salon that I opened on the Big Island of Hawaii. I wouldn't own Sanctuary without them and their amazing generosity and legacy. I have also learned so much from my mother and father, who are long-time business owners and entrepreneurs. My mother was a salon owner in the 80s, and she later sold her business to help run my father's business, making custom acoustic guitars.

I absolutely love being a salon owner and supporting stylists in achieving their goals of creating income and building their dream clientele. One of my passions within my business, for stylists and clients alike, is to cultivate a feeling of being seen, heard, and valued within Sanctuary Salon. To value others and have a "Spirit of Aloha" ("aloha" means mutual understanding and respect) within business is one of the largest impacts I hope I have brought with me from Hawaii to Nashville.

When you dream of being a salon owner, it's focused on the highlights, and it's not usually a smooth road—it's a constant process of growth and learning.

We've had flooding, backed-up shampoo bowls, electrical issues that we inherited with the businesses we purchased, and much more. As a business owner, I continue to learn how to practice gratitude and welcome change in the midst of chaos. It's constant.

We currently have a 12-station hybrid commission and booth rental salon. It's so exciting to dream and grow our largest salon in Nashville. Sanctuary Salon is a 12-station luxury salon. We focus on custom extensions, balayage, lived-in color, women's haircuts, and keratin treatments. We have stylists trained in luxury extensions, hair color, and haircut techniques.

We love bringing a "Spirit of Aloha" to Nashville and having clients feel seen, heard, and valued for their haircare services.

I can't wait to see what the future holds for Sanctuary Salon. I care deeply for each stylist who chooses to make Sanctuary their salon home as I pour my heart and dreams into my businesses.

Outside of work, I love spending time with my children. They are the biggest blessings I have been given on this earth, and I am thankful for each of their personalities.

Together, We Can Do It

Alexandra Watts & Annabelle Watts

Growing up in Kentucky, Annabelle and Alexandra Watts learned the value of hard work from their parents, which shaped their individual paths. Annabelle embraced music from a young age, mastering various instruments and later founding Grace Marketing Firm. Meanwhile, Alexandra pursued her passions through pageants, cheerleading, and eventually a career as a speech pathologist and Pure Barre instructor. Despite their differing interests, the sisters shared a love for creativity and unwavering support for each other. After college—Annabelle with a degree in integrated marketing communications and Alexandra in speech pathology—they combined their talents and launched Farrahline, an online boutique offering stylish clothing for women. Their entrepreneurial journey is a testament to their bond, determination, and the inspiration they've drawn from Nashville's dynamic energy. They hope their story encourages others to follow their dreams and embrace challenges with resilience. Explore their work at **farrahline.com**.

Instagram: @gracemarketingfirm & @shopfarrahline
Website: gracemarketingfirm.com & farrahline.com

——

"Together, we can do it."

I remember my sister Alexandra reassuring me as we grew up, watching our dad and mom work to support our family. At ten and seven years old, we often helped around the house, learning the value of hard work and determination. Our childhood experiences of witnessing our parents' dedication and hard work laid the groundwork for our own paths. Alexandra's encouragement during those early days became our guiding principle as we faced challenges and embarked on our own journeys into adulthood.

Growing up in Kentucky, my sister Alexandra and I shared similar interests but pursued different hobbies. I (Annabelle) started playing bluegrass music at age seven. Our father played guitar and banjo and our mother played the violin. After finding these instruments around the house, I began on the fiddle but soon picked up the guitar, mandolin, ukulele, and bass. I also started singing and songwriting.

Music became my passion. It was a way to express myself creatively, as well as connect with myself and with others. I took every chance I got to play music or sing for others. Alexandra, on the other hand, competed in pageants and cheerleading. From a young age, she was outgoing with a keen sense of fashion and an eye for design. She loved the stage, the excitement of a crowd's applause, and the creativity involved in designing her costumes and routines. Despite our different paths, our shared love for creativity and design kept us close as we were growing up. Though we had different interests, we were both the other's biggest supporters. "We rise by lifting others," our mom used to say, and Alexandra and I worked hard to lift each other to our fullest potential. Our high school years in Owensboro, Ky., were impactful, as they laid the foundation for our diverse interests and instilled in us the values of hard work, family values, creativity, and determination.

We both continued our education at The University of Mississippi. I graduated with a degree in integrated marketing communications (IMC), while Alexandra earned her degree in speech pathology. Our time in college was invaluable and taught us the skills we needed to pursue our respective careers. For me, the IMC program was a deep dive into the world of marketing, advertising, and public relations. I learned about the power of social media, the importance of branding, and how to identify and capitalize on emerging trends. Classes on digital marketing and consumer behavior taught me how to identify what's trending and what's not, and helped me understand how to connect with targeted consumer groups on a deeper level.

Alexandra's speech pathology program equipped her with the expertise to diagnose and treat communication disorders, but it also honed her empathy and patience. She learned how to build trust with her clients and adapt her methods to meet their individual needs. In college, Alexandra also grew in her love of fitness, and she became a Pure Barre instructor, where she applied the same principles of motivation and support to clients.

Though at first glance our studies seem disparate, both programs offered practical, hands-on experiences that allowed us to apply what we learned in real-world settings. We did not realize it at the time, but these experiences were crucial in shaping our career paths and gave us the confidence to pursue our shared entrepreneurial dreams.

After college, Alexandra started working as a speech-language pathologist and continued teaching Pure Barre classes. Her dedication and drive to succeed were evident in everything she did. She was always eager to learn and grow, both personally and professionally. For me, starting my own business was a long-held dream. I founded Grace Marketing Firm, which specializes in social media management, websites, branding, and print work. Creating this company was the realization of my dream to help businesses build strong digital presences. I used my skills in strategic communication and trend analysis to offer tailored solutions that met each client's unique needs. This entrepreneurial venture taught me the importance of adaptability, creativity, and the power of a cohesive brand story in achieving business success. Entrepreneurship was challenging but incredibly rewarding. I loved that it allowed me freedom and creativity but felt I wanted to do something bigger with my favorite partner, my sister.

After about a year of running Grace Marketing Firm, Alexandra and I decided to embark on a new venture together. We had always dreamed of opening a clothing store, so we launched an online boutique called Farrahline. Farrahline offers clothing for women of all ages. Running Farrahline together has been an amazing experience. I have often told others that if we can do it then you can do it. Yes, it is challenging to start a business. But matching a consumer need with a personal interest is incredibly rewarding. Moreover, this process has inspired both of us to support women-owned businesses. Together, Alexandra and I have combined our talents and passions into something meaningful that we can share with the public.

Living in Nashville has provided the perfect backdrop for our entrepreneurial journey. We absolutely love this city that we now call home. The city's vibrant culture and creative energy have inspired us and helped our businesses grow.

Our story is about the power of dreams and the strength of our sisterly bond. We've learned that the biggest obstacle to success is often just the fear of getting started. We've faced challenges, stumbled along the way, but we seem to always right ourselves, hand in hand, ready to conquer the next hurdle. No matter your age or the season of life you're in, we hope that our story can inspire others to take that leap of faith and pursue what you're passionate about. Alexandra and I are not just heroes in each other's eyes; we're heroes of our own story. We've built our businesses from the ground up, and we continue to inspire and uplift each other every day.

Please visit us at farrahline.com to see our unique collection and to connect with us. Our journey is far from over, and we're excited to see what the future holds, together. "Together, we can do it," indeed.

Closing:

Rewriting My Story, Turning Wounds into

Wisdom

Valentina Bain

Valentina is a holistic wellness expert with over 20 years of experience empowering clients to optimize their health and wellbeing. As an epigenetic coach, certified somatic therapist,

Emotion Code and EFT Master Practitioner, and reiki master, she takes an integrative approach to get to the root of imbalances.

After struggling for decades with her own chronic health issues, Valentina discovered Epigenetics, which allowed her to tackle personal health issues and apply this learning to help others. She now offers custom DNA, hormone, and mineral balancing blueprints, providing breakthrough protocols using advanced testing and mind-body techniques.

Valentina specializes in teaching clients how genetic variation informs the customized diet, lifestyle, and solutions that will lead each individual to their best self. By understanding how your body handles chemical processes, you can get right to the root of health issues.

As a trained practitioner, Valentina partners with clients to determine which genetic insights are most relevant, since expression evolves over time. She also incorporates somatic techniques to help release stored trauma and repattern neural pathways for emotional breakthroughs.

With compassion derived from her own health journey and as a natural-minded mom, Valentina is dedicated to helping others connect the dots to feel their healthiest and happiest. Learn more and discover your unique blueprint for optimization and a lifetime of elevated holistic healing and longevity at www.valentinabain.com or on IG @valentina.bain.

———

My journey has been filled with many twists and turns, yet each one has led me to where I am today—living my purpose and passion for empowering women to transform their health and live their dreams.

My earliest memories are of my struggles with chronic health issues. These were struggles that traditional medicine couldn't fully address; no matter how many doctors I visited or how many tests were ran, my symptoms just seemed to keep piling one on top of the next. In addition to all of my physical discomfort, I remember feeling this sense of being stuck and that I wasn't living the life I was meant to live from a young age.

Throughout school, I faced hurdles like learning disabilities that landed me in special schools, anxiety that made it almost impossible for me to make it through a full day of school, and even a thyroid disease diagnosis in my late teens. Although each health concern I faced was seen as separate, I grew curious...could they be related?

This early health rollercoaster ride sparked a deeper desire to understand my mind-body connection and set me on a path to uncover the root causes of health issues, years before I even knew what that was. While working at my first job at a gym in Atlanta, I got to know the trainers and watched them working with clients. I watched these clients walk into the gym looking and feeling one way, and just a few months (or for some just a few weeks) later, they would begin to visibly transform. They would talk about all the ways that their bodies were changing on the inside as well. This may seem obvious that the body could transform, but at 17 years old, it was all new to me. I started asking questions and changing my diet and lifestyle through their coaching. This became the beginning of my healing journey.

What started as a curious and personal quest to better understand my own health challenges grew into a bigger mission to help others find their way to well-being. I made it my motto at that time to *give my pain purpose*. This chapter of my life is when I began to study ancient healing modalities and learn how to eat and move to get healthier. It also sparked an intense interest in studying and understanding the mind-body connection and getting to the root cause of health issues, which has driven my entire career.

While the obstacles I faced in my earlier school years were difficult, they taught me very valuable lessons about perseverance and inner strength. My determination to overcome these challenges and find solutions fueled my drive to graduate early and pursue my dreams, no matter what stood in my way.

I overcame my learning disabilities and crippling anxiety in school through my determination to graduate early and follow my dreams. After a choir trip to Europe at age 14, the first seed was planted—I remember straying from the group, and peeking through a fence into a beautiful flower-filled courtyard garden and picturesque private cobblestone street. I don't know what it was about that place, but it struck a chord in me that I had never felt before. And just like that, I told myself that I would move to Paris one day.

The following year I became best friends with a German exchange student at my school. After getting my parents' permission, we made a plan to try to live together that year. I wrote a letter to the exchange organization to ask if she could live with my family due to the cultural disconnect at her original host family home. They said *yes*, and that was one of the happiest days of my life. We became soul sisters and spent every summer after that traveling in Europe together which helped me realize that my decision to move to Europe was exactly what my heart wanted. At age 17, I graduated high school and started a study abroad program in Paris. I had manifested my dream to move to Paris!

After my study abroad program, I found an international business school in Paris and made my move more permanent. It was incredible to go to school with so many people from other countries and travel somewhere new each weekend by train or a short flight. It was a magical chapter until I began getting stalked by a man I had briefly dated. I attempted to handle the situation alone—however, it continued to escalate. Eventually my parents encouraged me to come to the decision that leaving was the safest call. And just like that, my dream of living in Europe was placed on hold.

Although it was heartbreaking, it also expanded my perspective, and in hindsight, I know it led me exactly where I needed to go: back home to Atlanta, Ga. After my initial grief, I dove into my fascination around the mind-body connection and went to school to become a certified somatic practitioner. I began practicing medical massage, along with several other modalities such as craniosacral therapy, hydrotherapy, reiki, and BioResonance. I soaked up everything I could possibly learn from my incredible mentors who were making miracles happen every day and completely changing people's lives (including mine).

Once I began learning about the body, I couldn't stop the desire to study and share what I was learning. It honestly took over, and I found myself having conversations about health and healing with anyone who was interested. This passion for the body led me to become a labor doula and natural birth advocate. I began studying hypnobirthing and prenatal yoga, and I was able to put all of this knowledge to use as I became a mom at age 23. I had a beautiful two-hour labor and water-birthing experience with my daughter; little did I know that this tiny, incredible human would lead me to learn so much more.

I found myself deeply challenged when I discovered that my daughter had major gut health issues, along with other scary health concerns that again no doctor or test seemed to have the answers for (my natural medicine doctors didn't even know what was going on). I felt like I was reliving my past. My son was born a few years later with his own health puzzle; I then spent years in my own research until I began to unravel their issues one by one. This led me to a newfound passion for sharing all that I was learning to help other moms reverse their kids' chronic health issues naturally.

In 2008, the economy crashed, and my family lost everything. My parents got divorced after 35 years and my marriage shockingly ended shortly after. This opened the door for a painful, but massively transformational chapter. I felt led to embrace a fresh start and decided to sell all that I owned except for three outfits and my kids' favorite belongings. We moved from Georgia to California as official minimalists, and I began to once again practice all the healing tools that I knew...I felt I had no choice, as these were by far the darkest and scariest moments of my life! Becoming a single mom who understood the importance of healthy living and healing with very limited resources and so much stress, fueled my purpose. I became extremely passionate about empowering other women to break through abuse patterns, generational challenges, and subconscious blocks, so they could live their dreams, no matter what mountain was ahead.

These painful challenges pushed me into profound healing and the desire to rebuild an authentic life that I could love even more than I ever had before. I began saying "yes" to the aligned opportunities that flowed in. This led me to open four wellness businesses over seven years while going back to school for nutrition.

My greatest blessings through those years were learning the power of loving myself and trusting my intuition. After my divorce, I felt like my self-worth had plummeted and that my identity was shaken. I also became very mistrusting of my own self. Who would love me with my stretchmarks and my breasts that had just been nursing for four years?

I didn't even know how to love myself, and it was all tied to societal standards and perfectionism. I had read the work of Louise Hay and was familiar with mirror work and affirmations, and knew I wanted to learn how to fall in love with myself unconditionally—but I wasn't sure I knew what it even meant. So, I committed to a challenge of doing one act of self-love a day. I also committed to being more honest with myself than ever before. This included hard truths that I had to look in the mirror and own. I knew that my intuition had warned me of some red flags. After getting really honest with myself, I realized I had abandoned her, my own heart, inner navigation, and deeper knowing. If I wanted to honor my commitment to living authentically, then that meant in every area of life. I decided I wouldn't date until I could show up as me. I decided that any future partner must enter organically and make me feel safe to be myself. I also decided that no other relationship outside of myself was going to become my identity or determine my self-worth.

I found a deep peace and gratitude, realizing how much I could fall in love with myself and trust myself and how full of love and purpose my life was with my children, friends, family, and clients. I truly felt more complete than ever before.

My story took an unexpected turn in 2017. I remember it was a beautiful day and I felt particularly grateful and content, like there was a joyful skip in my step. It was a farmers' market night, and the park was filled with kids playing on the playground and vendors selling local goods. We were walking along the sidewalk when my children (ages six and nine at the time) saw a blue hammock hanging in the trees ahead. They began to run towards it, yelling back to ask me if it was ok if they asked to swing. As I began to tell them "no," I realized it was already too late. I felt so awkward and intrusive that my kids had interrupted the father and his boys sitting on their blanket reading next to their hammock. I walked up to my kids who had already asked permission and were joyfully jumping up to swing, and apologized for disturbing the family. Little did I know that this very moment would change my life and all of our lives forever!

After five years of healing myself, falling in love with myself, and only dating twice, I felt a chemistry I had never experienced before. There was definitely an attraction, but it was something more than that—I can only describe it as the feeling you get when you go home. His very presence felt comforting to my soul, like home to my heart. I didn't even know that a man could make me feel this way, yet I also didn't even know his name. This moment was made quite awkward by the fact that my mom was with me; I also had a single dad friend and his daughter beside me, so it appeared that I was with a boyfriend. We talked for a few minutes and then walked on past to the market not knowing if we would ever see each other again.

The farmers' market was not somewhere we went often, but the next week I decided I had to go back, and I thought really hard about what to wear in case I happened to see this man again at the park after thinking about him all week. As we arrived and I walked up to the park, there he was with his two boys at the playground. My heart lit up and my stomach had butterflies. Of course, my kids ran right over to say hello, and that day was the beginning of us. He had returned to find me too. We were all drawn together in this connection, unlike anything any of us had ever experienced before. We all had built-in besties as the kids' ages were very close, and they were kindred souls.

The adventures we shared and the depth of understanding and care that effortlessly flowed between us brought tremendous healing for us all. Against all odds, we blended our family of six beautifully like a modern day Brady bunch. I dreamed of having a big family, and they made that dream a reality. Still to this day, our family and the love we share is the greatest surprise of my life. This entire experience reminds me of the beauty of serendipity and the importance of trusting the timing of our paths and showing up open-hearted.

Opening my heart to the possibility of manifesting each of my dreams, even when achieving them seemed completely impossible, I believe opened doors in my mind and heart! My life now reflects visions I've held dear for decades: thriving health, a beautiful home filled with love, a soulmate partnership, sharing deep bonds with my children, a business that ignites hope in others, traveling the world, and even collaborating on this book. My life has taught me that boldly daring to dream, taking aligned action, and trusting in forces greater than ourselves can make life magically unfold further than we can even imagine.

My life and passions were all on track until a concussion in 2023 forced me to a halt. It took six months to fully recover. I found myself face-to-face with painful childhood truths and trauma surfacing in my dreams, and I knew it was an opportunity to heal yet again. I used this period to work through those past wounds and began making peace with my past; while using this chapter as a catalyst to explore and learn other trauma healing modalities. This personal journey allowed me to better support others in their healing processes and deepened my empathy in many ways.

Though the road twisted and turned, embracing each challenge as a powerful opportunity for growth has shaped me into who I am today. By turning wounds into wisdom, we rewrite our stories, but we also light the way for others to do the same for generations to come.

Leaning into pain allows healing light and love to shine through the cracks. I believe that's how we can truly change the world: by being vulnerable enough to let our light shine.

I'm grateful this path led me to you. May you courageously step into your next chapter. Trust in the unknown, follow your intuition, and envision your wildest dreams. Stay open to how they may manifest in astonishing and beautiful ways. You are the author of your story and it's not over yet so there's always time for a plot twist. Make it legendary!

About the Curator, Leigh M. Clark

Four-time best-selling author Leigh M. Clark is known for her inspiring books, including *The Dream is in Your Hands*, *Living Kindly*, and the *Slay the USA* series. Her work as an author has empowered and motivated countless readers by highlighting kindness, resilience, and the strength of community. In addition to her writing career, Leigh has over 20 years of experience as a business strategist, working with Fortune 500 companies to help them grow and succeed.

Leigh's latest project, the Slay the USA series, is a growing national movement that shines a spotlight on extraordinary women across the country who are leaving their mark on their communities and industries. Through this series, Leigh is empowering these women to share their stories of triumph, leadership, and impact, much like she has done in her own life. The series is rapidly expanding, highlighting women in cities from coast to coast, celebrating their contributions and inspiring others to follow their lead.

Leigh's expertise and passion for leadership and empowerment have made her a sought-after speaker, with multiple appearances on the TEDx stage. Her stories of kindness and personal growth have been featured in prominent publications like *HuffPost* and shared through appearances on *The Today Show* and the *Rachael Ray Show*.

As the founder of Kindleigh, a movement focused on giving back through acts of kindness, Leigh has led initiatives that have raised significant funds for charitable causes. Her mission is to create lasting change through kindness and sharing stories of impact, further solidifying her role as a leader in philanthropy.

Leigh resides in Southwest Florida with her son, Carter, and the love of her life. She's here to make an impact and leave her mark by illuminating others.

"Don't let the world change your heart. Let your heart change the world." - Leigh M. Clark

IG: @leighmclark @slaytheusa

www.leighmclark.com

www.slaytheusa.com